What Life Was Like

IN THE AGE OF CHIVALRY

Medieval Europe
AD 800 ~ 1500

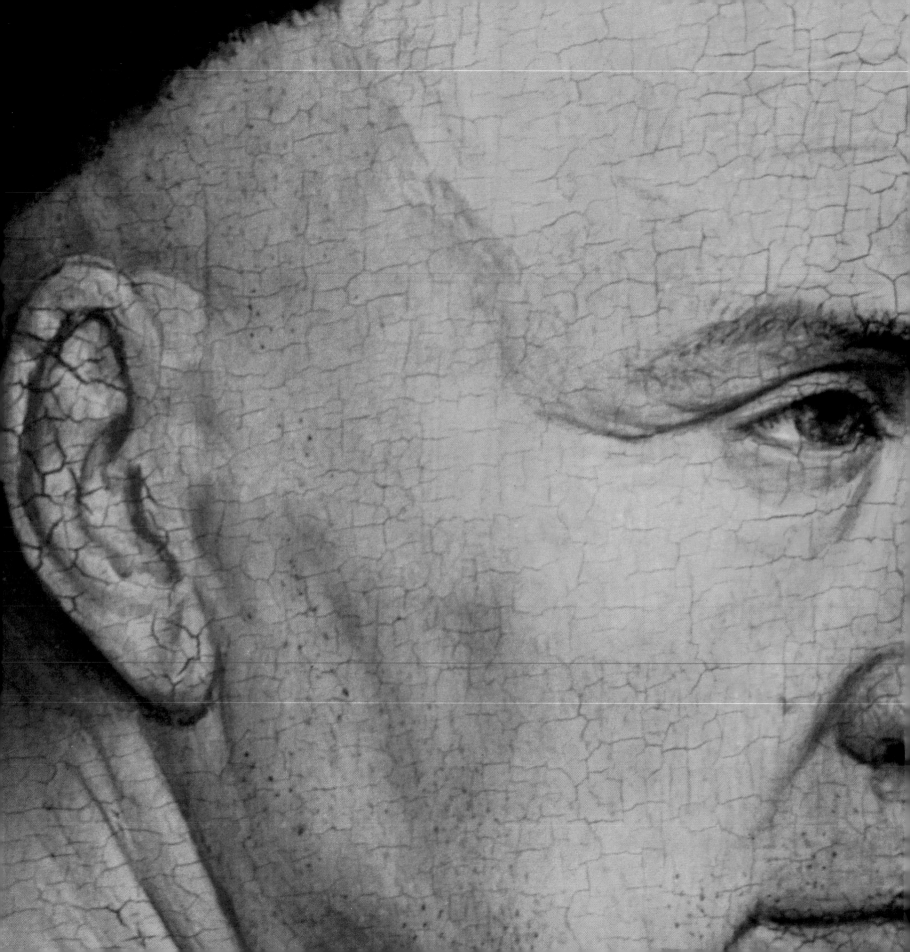

What Life Was Like

IN THE AGE OF CHIVALRY

Medieval Europe
AD 800 – 1500

BY THE EDITORS OF TIME-LIFE BOOKS, ALEXANDRIA, VIRGINIA

CONTENTS

From Roman Rule to the Renaissance:
Overview and Timeline   8

1

In the Service of God   14

2

Loyal Men and True   50

3

To the Manor Born   88

4

Of Towns and Tradesmen   120

ESSAYS

Monastic Life   42

In God's Name: The Crusades   79

A Child's World   113

Cathedrals: For the Glory of God   148

GLOSSARY   158
PICTURE CREDITS   161
ACKNOWLEDGMENTS   162
BIBLIOGRAPHY   162
INDEX   165

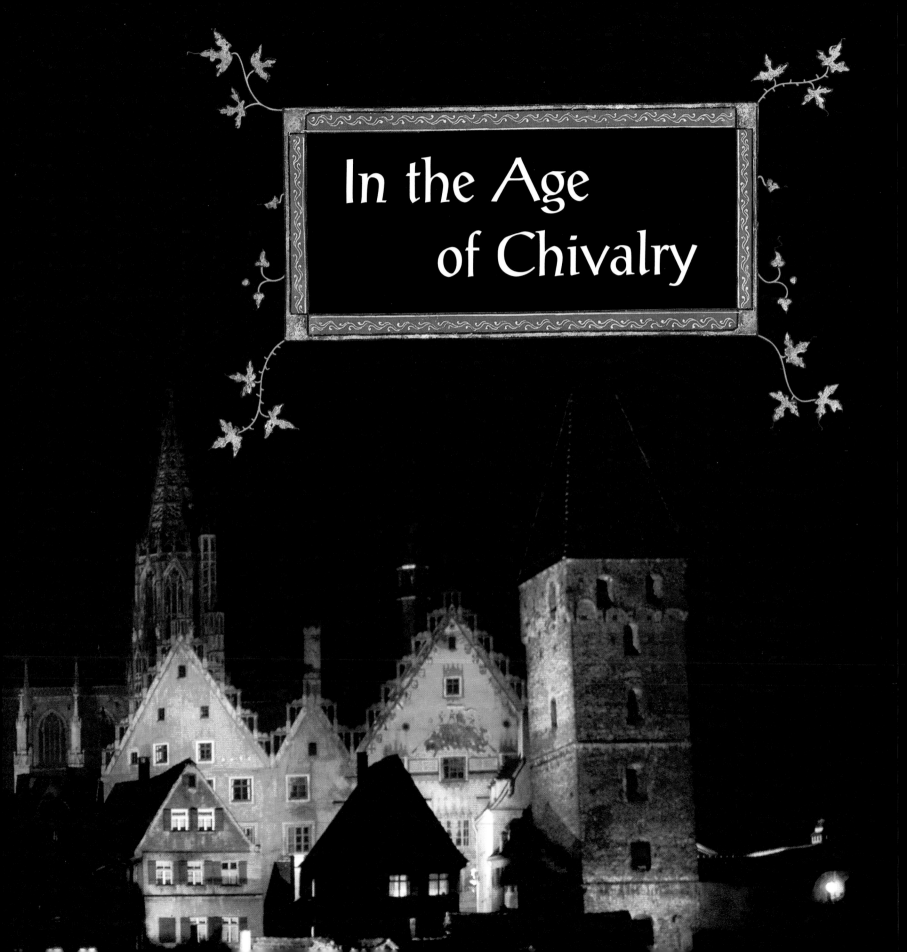

In the Age
of Chivalry

From Roman Rule to the Renaissance

When the Visigoths sacked Rome in AD 410, shock waves rippled throughout the European continent. The Caesars had bound Europe's diverse and far-flung provinces to Rome's central authority by establishing military outposts and a trade network stretching from northern England and Germany to every shore of the Mediterranean. The empire had also provided a common currency and language, Latin. But with the fall of Rome, the physical legacy of the empire—an extensive array of paved roads, aqueducts, and administrative towns—began to decay. Europe's government degenerated into a patchwork of small kingdoms and tribal states constantly warring with their neighbors over land and power. Long-distance trade dried up.

In this economic and political void, a new system based on the manor developed. The vast majority of Europe's population lived in small, self-sufficient communities as peasant farmers—or serfs—bound to the local lord. Though not slaves in the strict sense, these serfs worked their master's fields and also owed him a share of the harvest from their own. In return, the lord provided them with housing, farm animals, and perhaps most important, protection from rov-

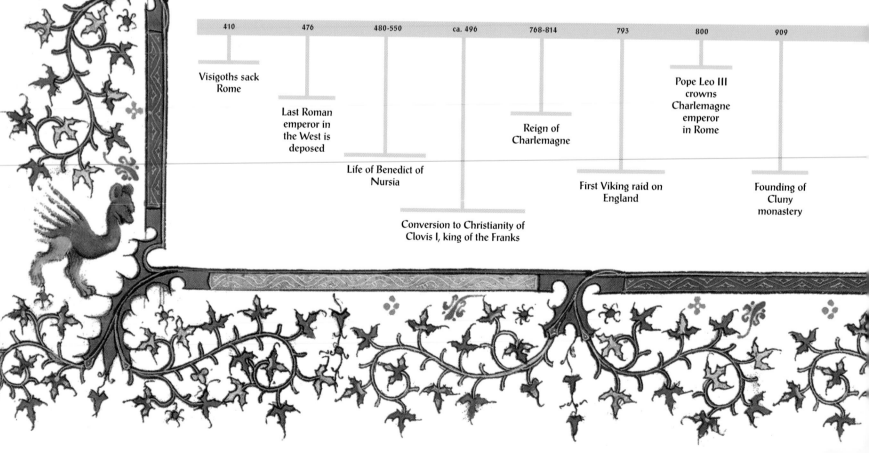

| 410 | 476 | 480-550 | ca. 496 | 768-814 | 793 | 800 | 909 |

Visigoths sack Rome

Last Roman emperor in the West is deposed

Life of Benedict of Nursia

Conversion to Christianity of Clovis I, king of the Franks

Reign of Charlemagne

First Viking raid on England

Pope Leo III crowns Charlemagne emperor in Rome

Founding of Cluny monastery

ing bands of brigands and from the threat of foreign invasion.

Possession of the manorial estates was often given to soldiers who, having sworn allegiance to their lords, enjoyed the profits as payment for their military service. In time men-of-arms would become known as knights, and an elaborate code of ethics—known as chivalry—would govern their actions both on and off the battlefield. Through valorous service to their lords and booty garnered in tournaments with their peers, many knights became rich and powerful landowners in their own right.

Throughout this early period, sometimes called the Dark Ages, one remaining vestige of the time of the Roman Empire, the Catholic Church, sought to reunify Europe, both spiritually and politically. Knowing the influence a lord could have on his vassals, the church sent missionaries to the nobility. The missionaries enjoyed great success in winning local rulers over to their faith, most notably Clovis I, king of the Franks, in about 496, and the influential King Ethelbert of Kent in 597. Ethelbert's capital, Canterbury, would become the spiritual seat of the English church.

Catholic monasteries sprang up throughout western Europe. In the sixth century, the Italian monk Benedict of Nursia composed a set of tenets that were embraced by subsequent practitioners of monasticism. The Benedictine Rule emphasized a simple, but busy, life, devoid of luxuries and devoted to study, prayer, and manual labor. The monasteries were not only strongholds of faith but also the principal centers of learning, and many parents placed one or more of their children under the monks' care in what was in fact a lifetime contract.

To cope with the ever-expanding numbers of the faithful, the Catholic Church developed an enormous bureaucracy—with

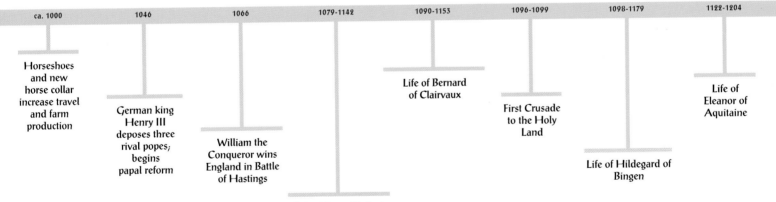

| ca. 1000 | 1046 | 1066 | 1079-1142 | 1090-1153 | 1096-1099 | 1098-1179 | 1122-1204 |

Horseshoes and new horse collar increase travel and farm production

German king Henry III deposes three rival popes; begins papal reform

William the Conqueror wins England in Battle of Hastings

Life of Peter Abelard

Life of Bernard of Clairvaux

First Crusade to the Holy Land

Life of Hildegard of Bingen

Life of Eleanor of Aquitaine

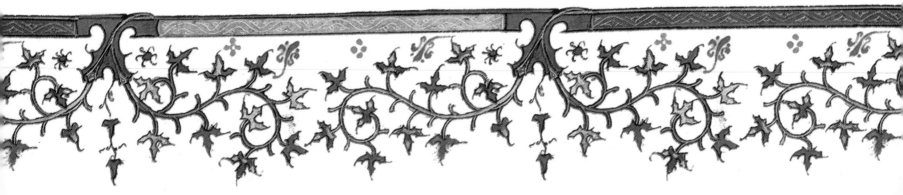

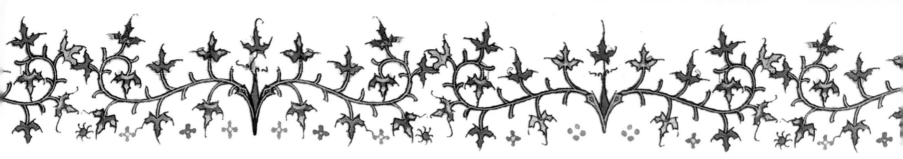

the pope at its head—to run its administrative, financial, and spiritual affairs. And it soon cast an ambitious eye on the political arena as well. In AD 800 Pope Leo III crowned the king of the Franks, Charlemagne, as emperor, firmly establishing the church's role in affairs of state.

Under Charlemagne, the heart of western Europe was united as never before, with one strong and effective secular ruler and one official faith. Although the great king's domain was partitioned after his death and never again approached the grandeur that existed in his day, the Catholic Church continued to play a prominent and sometimes antagonistic role in politics with Charlemagne's successors.

The 11th through the 13th centuries was a period of dramatic change and progress. Technological advancements in agriculture, such as windmills and improved harnesses for draft an-

imals, coupled with the cultivation of crops high in protein created a population explosion in Europe. Agricultural surpluses freed increasing numbers of people to move to urban areas, causing spectacular growth in the size of European cities.

The backbone of Europe's urban revitalization was a new economic rank—the merchant class. Many of these businessmen were former serfs who had started out as peddlers selling simple necessities from village to village. Then, as the cities—and the standard of living—grew, some of this group went on to amass great fortunes and to become the cities' ruling class as well. Education became very important to these new middle and upper classes; universities eventually emerged from informal clusters of teachers and began issuing degrees in specialized subjects such as law and medicine.

The next two centuries, however, would bring grave rever-

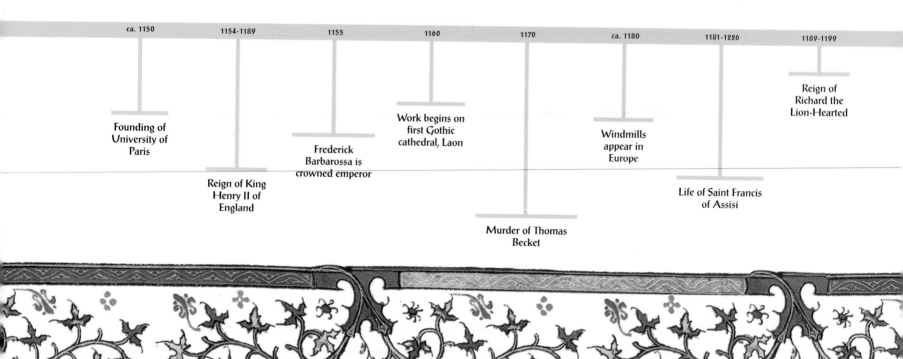

ca. 1150 — Founding of University of Paris

1154-1189 — Reign of King Henry II of England

1155 — Frederick Barbarossa is crowned emperor

1160 — Work begins on first Gothic cathedral, Laon

1170 — Murder of Thomas Becket

ca. 1180 — Windmills appear in Europe

1181-1226 — Life of Saint Francis of Assisi

1189-1199 — Reign of Richard the Lion-Hearted

sals to this era of growth and prosperity. Though the threat of external invasion had faded, the nation-states of Europe continued to make war on each other—often with disastrous results. And nature itself would deliver the most devastating blow of all—an outbreak of bubonic plague that cut like a scythe through Europe's cities and countryside, killing tens of millions.

In the wake of these calamities, people became increasingly disaffected with the social institutions of the day. The church's constant meddling in secular affairs, for example, would eventually produce a backlash in the region north of the Alps. As papal authority waned and hostility toward the wealth and privilege of the church increased, Christian piety would become more individualistic, resulting in large-scale religious reformation. And in Italy, a movement—calling itself humanist—would produce the great cultural flowering of the Renaissance. Looking to classical Greece and Rome for inspiration, these humanists scornfully referred to the intervening thousand years as the Middle Ages.

Though the humanists used the term derisively, the Middle Ages was a dynamic era, distinguished by many important political, economic, social, and cultural changes and innovations, and the period provided the foundation for the incredible achievements of the Renaissance. In the ensuing chapters, the compelling stories of medieval people will reveal the depth of the age's faith, the complexity and purity of its ideals, the grandeur of its art, and what life was like.

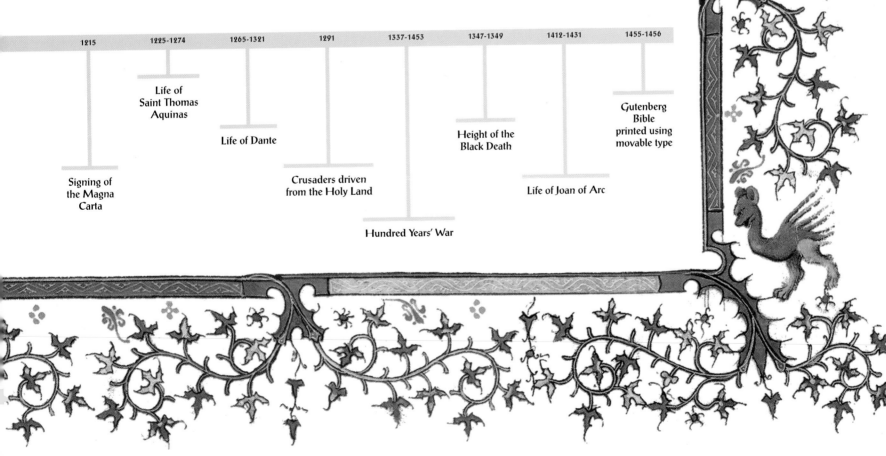

| 1215 | 1225-1274 | 1265-1321 | 1291 | 1337-1453 | 1347-1349 | 1412-1431 | 1455-1456 |

Life of Saint Thomas Aquinas

Life of Dante

Height of the Black Death

Gutenberg Bible printed using movable type

Signing of the Magna Carta

Crusaders driven from the Holy Land

Life of Joan of Arc

Hundred Years' War

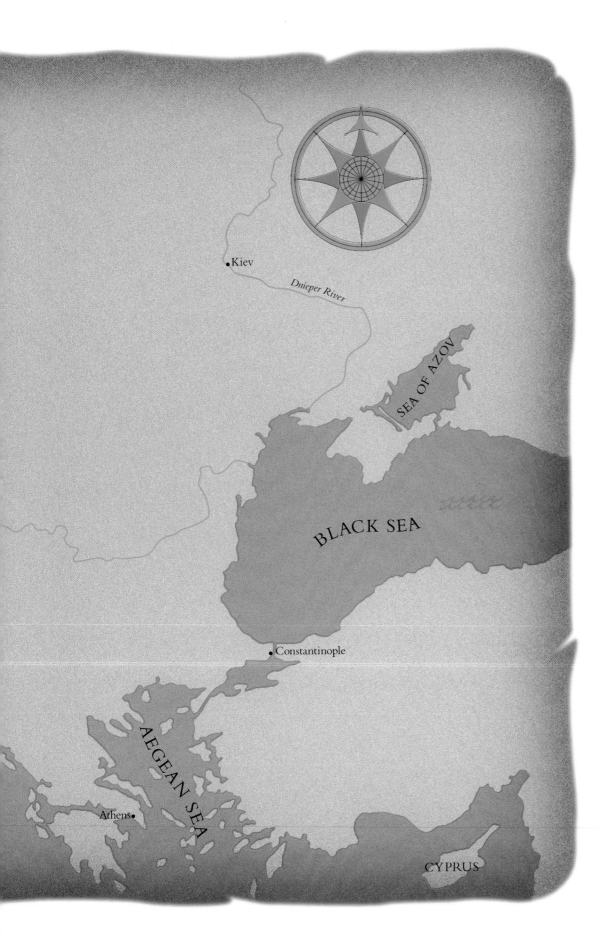

Much of the area shown on this map—from York in the north to Augsburg in the east and all of the land bordering the Mediterranean Sea—was controlled by the Roman Empire. With the fall of Rome in the fifth century AD, Europe dissolved into a jumble of local kingdoms and principalities too small to show on a map of this scale.

During the first half of the Middle Ages, the threat of foreign invasion was ever present. Muslim armies from northern Africa conquered Spain and pushed into France. Fierce nomads from the distant steppes of central Asia periodically swept in, spreading terror and mayhem. And Norsemen from Scandinavia conducted destructive raids on the coastal regions of northern Europe.

In AD 800 much of western Europe achieved political unity under Charlemagne. Charlemagne's empire did not long outlive him, however; his realm was partitioned after his death, and borders remained fluid for the rest of the medieval period. But Charlemagne's conquests defined the area as a cultural unit, and he became known as the Father of Europe. Some of the more famous kingdoms of this later era are listed on the map at left. Many of these names have survived as provinces in modern-day European states.

CHAPTER ONE

In the Service of God

Pope Leo III crowns Charlemagne emperor at Saint Peter's basilica in Rome on Christmas Day in the year 800. The coronation sealed the alliance between the papacy and Charlemagne, thrusting the Frankish king into the role of secular head of western Christendom.

he city of Rome awoke on Christmas morning in the year AD 800 to a blessed, newly established state of peace. Though the eternal city was no longer the hub of a mighty empire, it still glowed with the majesty of its own past. Visitors who streamed into town to celebrate the birth of Jesus gazed in awe at the impressive array of majestic monuments, colonnaded buildings, and soaring, arched aqueducts that the city's engineers struggled to keep in working order. Surviving fragments of architecture from the time of the Caesars had been incorporated into some of the 300 houses of worship controlled by Rome's current rulers—the popes of the Catholic Church.

Atop the Vatican—one of the city's fabled seven hills—in a comfortable bungalow next to the basilica of Saint Peter, the man responsible for Rome's peace had also awakened. Charlemagne, the king of the Franks, had traveled 700 miles from his capital of Aachen in northwest Germany to celebrate Christmas Mass with Pope Leo III. As he prepared for the service, the king groused to his servants about the attire they had laid out for him. He had intended to wear the traditional Frankish cloth-of-gold suit—a knee-length tunic with long stockings and colorful bands of cloth wrapped around the legs—that was reserved for such important occasions. But Leo had urged him to don a long Roman toga and to fasten across his broad shoulders the accompanying cloak of Greek origin known as the chlamys. Charlemagne had reluctantly yielded to the pope's wishes. He secured the golden belt that encircled his waist and slipped into sandals gleaming with precious stones. Though he may have felt uncomfortable in this garb, he mustered his dignity and strode regally out of his chambers to head the procession of Frankish nobles to Saint Peter's.

Charlemagne entered the magnificent basilica, where Leo greeted him warmly and led him to the altar near the vault holding Saint Peter's earthly remains. The huge church was packed with Roman dignitaries, who, as they followed the liturgy of the mass, secretly fixed their eyes upon the graying, once golden-haired Frankish monarch. At six

"We have written this Rule that by observing it in monasteries, we may show ourselves to have some degree of goodness in life and a beginning of holiness." So declared Saint Benedict of the decree that he hands to a group of monks in the illustration above.

Written in 529 and considered by some the greatest single document of the Middle Ages, the Benedictine Rule became the guiding principle for Western monasticism. Adopted by hundreds of monasteries throughout Europe, the Rule had so great an impact that the 400-year period after it was written has been called the Benedictine Age. In some cases, though, it pitted monks against each other; using Benedict's dictates, the Dominican "black friars" *(left)* and Franciscan "gray friars" *(right)* sought to challenge the wealth and laxity of older monastic orders.

feet four inches, he towered above his fellow worshipers. His devotion was revealed in the furrow of his brow and the tautness of his thin lips, above which a long, full mustache sagged onto the cheeks of a round, beardless face.

As the mass drew to a close, Leo arose, walked up to Charlemagne, and placed upon his head a dazzling crown of gold studded with precious jewels. Then he led the congregation in chanting: "To Carolus Augustus, crowned by God, great and peace-giving Emperor of the Romans, life and victory." These words were proclaimed three times before Leo dropped to the floor and kissed the hem of Charlemagne's toga. Then the pope anointed him with holy oil, and Charlemagne graciously accepted the exalted title, while offering gifts of his own to the church.

Leo became the first pope ever to crown an emperor. Some would maintain, however, that he had acted without informing anyone—including Charlemagne—in advance. His motives were twofold: a very real sense of gratitude to the Frankish king for past services and a desire to fix the Catholic Church's role in the secular affairs of Europe's monarchies.

It was no exaggeration to say that Leo owed his life to Charlemagne. Leo had had problems right from the start of his reign five years earlier. He was accused of immorality and simony—the sale of positions of authority in the church—and was entangled in a dispute over papal lands that were coveted by local lords. Matters came to a head on an April day in 799: As Leo was marching through the streets of Rome in a procession, he was suddenly thrown to the ground by several knife-bearing noblemen, who tried to cut out his tongue and gouge out his eyes. The pope managed to get away and

flee north into Charlemagne's territory, which by that time encompassed a large portion of western Europe. There, under the king's protection, he regained his sight, although his eyelids still bore thin white scars.

In response to Leo's pleas for aid, Charlemagne had brought an army to Rome in November and quickly disposed of the pope's enemies. Once order was restored, the king assembled a group of churchmen, nobles, and his own warriors, before whom Leo was compelled to swear his innocence. Charlemagne apparently considered the matter settled. By virtue of both his personal piety and the forced conversion of his new subjects to the Ro-

man Catholic faith, he had already earned the church's approval. Now he had the pope's personal gratitude as well. But Leo may also have had the church's future interests in mind when he arranged Charlemagne's coronation.

With the collapse of the Roman Empire four centuries earlier, the stability imposed by Roman legions had dissolved and the public works projects—roads, aqueducts, and reservoirs—built and maintained by the empire had fallen into disrepair. During these chaotic times, which have come to be known as the Dark Ages, Europe had experienced a decline of law, education, building, and commerce. Out of this political and spiritual vacuum, two forces had gradually emerged: a collection of minor kingdoms north of the Alps that constantly vied with each other for power and territory, and Catholicism, which had by Leo's day become the dominant religion in western Europe.

The Catholic Church had developed a far-reaching bureaucracy with the pope at the top. Below him were the archbishops, bishops, canons, abbots, monks, nuns, and the village priests, who were the citizenry's direct and most accessible link to the entire chain. Under this system the church had acquired valuable holdings—manor houses, abbeys, and their accompanying agricultural lands—in every province, and touched the

ILLUMINATED MANUSCRIPTS

Besides their spiritual and charitable duties, medieval monks spent much of their time with quill in hand, copying onto parchment religious works as well as treatises on medicine, astronomy, and law. Particular care and attention were paid to illustrating these texts with enlarged, magnificently drawn opening letters, called illuminations; the example at left shows a monk buying parchment from a trader. At far left, the interior of an initial—from the 12th-century Winchester Bible—portrays the prophet Elijah talking with King Ahaziah, and below that, depicts the prophet ascending into heaven in a chariot.

lives of the lowliest peasants. Now that Charlemagne had conquered and united most of Europe's individual kingdoms, Leo foresaw an expanded role for the church within Charlemagne's realm. Perhaps the best measure of the church's success is that, by the middle of the 12th century, Charlemagne's domain became known as the Holy Roman Empire.

The era of Charlemagne and his successors—now known as the medieval period, or the Middles Ages—would bring great change to Europeans in all walks of life. Ordinary people would discover new avenues of escape from the virtual slavery of the ironhanded system that tied them to a parcel of land and left their fate to the whims of their manor lord. Kings and queens would clash in bloody, drawn-out wars. The sacred realm of monasteries and convents was the scene of large-scale human drama, where men and women would wrestle with the competing demands of body and spirit. Caught up in the turbulence of the times were persons as diverse as Gottschalk, who was tried for heresy; Abelard and Heloise, who surrendered to passions that brought forth a terrible retribution; and the charismatic Bernard, who was destined to become a saint, but was seldom to encounter humans that lived up to his ideals.

Although monastic life once meant a withdrawal from earthly pursuits, by the ninth century, monasteries and convents had become a major force in the secular world of agriculture and government. Often located in populated areas, these religious houses were founded by the feudal lords of great estates, who sought credit from a divine source, status among their neighbors, and a convenient place to settle relatives. These aristocrats reserved for themselves the right to choose the abbot—the highest governing official. They usually appointed their own sons or, in the case of abbess, daughters.

Starting out with lands and treasure donated by these patrons, religious houses became wealthy estates in their own right, pos-

sessing huge stores of grain and wine, and overseeing throngs of agricultural and domestic workers. Some abbeys owned as many as 3,000 manor houses, and one had 20,000 people living on its vast holdings. The abbot of a large monastery was therefore among the most powerful men in the kingdom, and some could influence the pope.

Charlemagne himself insisted that monasteries make education a priority, for he valued learning with the passion of a man deprived of its benefits. Like many a warrior brought up to grasp the nuances of swordplay rather than wordplay, he regretted his lack of full literacy. Though he could speak Latin and understand Greek, try as he might he was unable to make the letters of the alphabet to his satisfaction. This may have been why, in 789, he decreed that every monastery was to maintain a school to teach young men to read and write, do arithmetic, and study both religious works and the classics. He also encouraged the development of a standard script with clearly formed letters to replace the jumble of scripts then in existence, many scarcely legible.

The monks and nuns who were to undertake the task of education came largely from the upper classes. But the majority of them had not chosen this career themselves. Most had been placed in religious houses as children by their parents. These youthful initiates—known as oblates—typically were the second sons or younger offspring of either sex born to a large family. As such, they could not expect a substantial inheritance or dowry, but might find power and prestige in the service of the church.

Such a youth was Gottschalk, the son of a Saxon count. Born in 804, he was given over to the influential monastery at Fulda in central Germany at around the age of seven, the typical age for accepting oblates. On the day that Gottschalk entered the monastery, his mother and father, following the accepted practice, brought him to the altar during mass. Solemnly his parents wrapped his right hand in the altar cloth, kissed it, and offered it to the priest, who took the proffered hand and made the sign of the cross over the boy's head. Gottschalk was then turned over to the abbot, who poured holy water on his head and cut his hair, while the cantor chanted prayers.

After mass the parents left and the young boy was ceremonially stripped of his clothes. He then put on a black, knee-length, shapeless outer garment that hung loosely from his shoulders and had a sewn-in hood or cowl. He would wear a garment such as this daily for the rest of his life. He would slip it over a simple tunic, donning a heavier one in cooler weather. A belt, stockings, and shoes or sandals completed his outfit. In the long, cold Saxon winters, Gottschalk would also wear heavy woolen pants.

The abbey also issued him a reed mattress and pillow, a linen sheet, a wool blanket, and a knife. Gottschalk and his fellow monks were strictly forbidden to possess personal property and could be severely punished if caught. The abbot himself searched their quarters for any sign of private possessions.

As the son of a wealthy nobleman, Gottschalk had probably led a rather pampered existence at home. But from the day he entered the monastery, that life was over. From now on, all his daily routines—in fact, every aspect of his life—would be governed by the Benedictine Rule, a set of dictates created by Saint Benedict of Nursia, the sixth-century abbot who founded a group of monastic houses that later gave rise to the order that bears his name.

Charlemagne had decreed that the Benedictine Rule become the standard for all monasteries and convents. The Rule dictated a day spent in prayer, study, and work, ordering the hours into a rigid schedule.

Gottschalk was awakened in his dormitory each day by the sound of the abbey bells sometime between midnight and two a.m. Yawning and shivering, Gottschalk and the other young monks slipped on their clothes and, in rows, marched—or perhaps stumbled—to the chapel. In the darkened choir, lit only by the glow of a few candles that cast flickering shadows over the hooded figures, they chanted matins—three hymns, three psalms, and three lessons—followed by lauds, the next prescribed series of prayers. After a brief nap, they would pray again at the break of dawn, and at three-hour intervals throughout the day.

It was not until two in the afternoon that Gottschalk had his first meal of the day. In winter it was his only meal of the day, but with the longer days of summer he was also permitted a light supper after evening vespers. There was seldom a shortage of food at Fulda, and every day Gottschalk could drink his fill of ale or wine, sometimes spiced with herbs, and eat bread, cheese, porridge, and deliciously seasoned dishes of fish, veg-

Seen here with a fellow monk, the English scholar Alcuin *(above, right)* instituted many of Charlemagne's cultural reforms.

etables, and eggs. Although meat was forbidden under the Benedictine Rule, ailing monks were exempt, and in some religious houses it was said that half the monks would report sick to enjoy a feast of meat in the infirmary.

Seated at the long wooden table, Gottschalk absorbed the intricacies of table etiquette, such as raising his goblet in unison with the other monks and bowing before taking a sip. While the dining hall in his father's manor house was decidedly boisterous on occasion, mealtime at the monastery was shrouded in silence, as demanded by the Rule. To communicate, Gottschalk had to learn the peculiar sign language that the monks had developed. If he wanted fish at dinner, for example, he made swimming motions with his hands; for cheese, he would press his palms together. To indicate the word, "hot," he held the side of his right forefinger in his closed mouth.

Gottschalk was assigned to the care of a small group of masters. Like other young monks, he was constantly watched by a master and could be flogged for even minor infractions of the rules, such as falling asleep during psalms or rising from his seat too slowly at matins. In the dormitory Gottschalk was surrounded by these vigilant monks, who slept between every two boys. In the bathhouse, too, masters stood between each pair of boys as the young oblates washed their hands and faces at the basins, which they were required to do several times a day. Rules even prescribed the specific times when the monks were allowed to relieve themselves. On Saturday a thorough washing was required, while full baths were decreed for Christmas and Easter. Shaving was also regularly scheduled, the monks sitting on facing rows of benches, singing psalms as they shaved each other's beards.

A UNIFORM SCRIPT

Although he was barely able to scratch his own name, Charlemagne promoted learning and scholarship throughout his empire. Among his reforms was the adoption of a written Latin script, known as the Carolingian script, or the Caroline minuscule. Later used in the first printing presses, its elegant, rounded letter forms would become the basis of our modern script.

The eighth-century manuscript shown at left, an excerpt from the Gospel of Matthew, illustrates some distinctly modern elements of the Carolingian script, highlighted below: the ampersand, which comes from *et*–Latin for "and"–and the use of abbreviations, such as the shortening of *dominus*–"Lord," or "God"–to *ds.*

Gottschalk was required to be a watcher himself, and an informer as well, telling his masters immediately whenever he spotted another boy misbehaving—one favorite prank was to drip hot candle wax on the shaved pate of colleagues who dozed off during a service. If he failed to make such a report, and the rule breaker was discovered, both Gottschalk and the culprit would be beaten. Perhaps he was not as severely restricted as the youngsters of another monastery, whose rules decreed that no boy "ever presume to make any sign or even to wink his eye at another youth, or to smile at him or simulate any familiarity, or even sit so that their faces are turned towards each other." Such constraints no doubt prevented a great deal of mischief-making, but they also made it difficult to forge friendships.

Any shortcomings in Gottschalk's behavior were brought up at the daily meeting, which all monks were required to attend in the chapter house, so named because these lively sessions always began by reading a chapter of the Rule. After a discussion of business matters, such as rents or supplies, attention turned to moral questions. Individuals had to confess their faults, or have them noted by others, and orders were given for their correction.

In a small schoolroom Gottschalk and his classmates labored over their daily lessons. Their first task was to learn Latin,

THE MYSTICAL VISIONS OF HILDEGARD

In the midst of an era that accorded women few opportunities and even less acclaim, the German abbess Hildegard von Bingen defied tradition. Mystic, poet, scientist, painter, healer, prophet, preacher, musician, and social critic, this "simple creature," as she described herself, became one of the most remarkable figures of medieval Europe.

Hildegard was born in 1098 to a noble family that lived near the cathedral city of Mainz, on the Rhine River. At the age of three, Hildegard began experiencing prophetic visions accompanied by a dazzling light. Perhaps for this reason, Hildegard's parents turned her care and education over to a holy woman named Jutta, who led a women's cloister at a local Benedictine abbey. Jutta taught her well, and upon Jutta's death, Hildegard, at age 38, became the abbess.

Unsure of the origin of her visions, Hildegard had told few

Hildegard's convent in Rupertsberg dominates a hilly site overlooking the Rhine River.

people about them. But after becoming abbess, she had a vision that changed her life. "The heavens were opened and a blinding light of exceptional brilliance flowed through my entire brain," she wrote. And God commanded her: "Write what you see and hear." With great reluctance, she began to describe her revelations, elaborately detailed images that dealt with such subjects as the fall of Lucifer, the Creation, and the Last Judgment.

"My consciousness had been transformed," she later wrote about this period, "as if I no longer knew myself, as if raindrops were falling from the hand of God upon my soul." But countless others were eager to

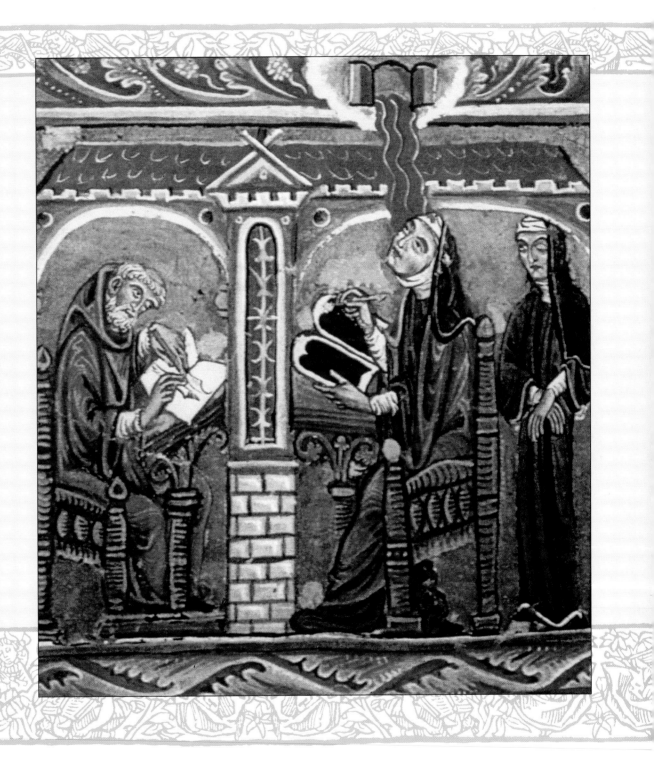

"Inflamed by a fiery light," Hildegard records a vision on a wax tablet with a stylus. She is attended by a nun and a monk who stands ready to make a parchment copy of the vision.

23

know her. After she received official church approval of her writings, in fact, her divine insights were sought by the great leaders of the day, among them four popes, two emperors, monarchs like Eleanor of Aquitaine and Henry II of England, and church prelates like Thomas Becket and Bernard of Clairvaux.

In 1150 Hildegard relocated her nuns to Rupertsberg, on the banks of the Rhine near the town of Bingen. The convent prospered, and she founded another one across the river, commuting regularly between them. The visions that she claimed to see in life were apparently shared by many upon her death: On the day she died, at age 81, brilliant crosses and circles were said to illuminate the skies, as if the visionary were bequeathing her followers their own glimpse of the heavenly kingdom.

Encircled by a heavenly embrace, man stands at the center of the cosmos in one of Hildegard's visions.

Although untutored in musical composition, Hildegard wrote around 75 songs; one of which is shown at right. Such divinely inspired music, she believed, recaptured the joys of paradise.

In Hildegard's vision of creation, the "finger of God" brings forth life on earth *(center)* while Christ emerges from Mary's womb *(bottom)*.

since all the other subjects were taught in that language. As he struggled to master the complexities of Latin grammar, Gottschalk took notes by impressing the point of a wooden stylus into the surface of a wax tablet. Later he would carefully copy these notes onto a sheet of parchment. He read ancient Roman fables as well as biblical proverbs and expanded his vocabulary by studying glossaries of words.

Arithmetic was taught in the form of word problems, but the use of Roman numerals made it somewhat difficult to do complex sums. Apparently Gottschalk proved to be an able scholar, for he was sent to complete his studies with the prestigious instructors at the monastery of Reichenau, on Lake Constance in southern Germany. Had the masters at Fulda known how this higher education would influence Gottschalk, they might not have sent him. For the young monk emerged from Reichenau as what in those days was a rare commodity: a free thinker. And he would soon become a thorn in the side of the Catholic hierarchy.

Many monks found satisfaction in the unquestioning obedience of monastic life, the feeling of belonging to a tight-knit community, and the dedication to a lofty purpose. But Gottschalk, by the age of 25, felt himself drawn in a different direction. He longed to participate in the kind of unconfined academic and religious discus-

Most patients lie two to a bed in this
French hospital, which, like many
medieval hospitals, was run by nuns
or monks for the benefit of the poor.

sions that were only possible outside the walls of the abbey.

In 829 Gottschalk wrote to the council of bishops in Mainz, asking for his release from the monastery. He asserted that his father had had no right to consign him at the age of seven to a lifelong compact. But his abbot at Fulda, Hrabanus Maurus, argued that "it was lawful for a Christian man to dedicate his offspring to God in religion; that a vow vowed unto God could not be broken without great sin." After much debate, the council sided with the persuasive young monk, but such was Maurus's influence that Gottschalk, rather than obtaining his outright freedom, was merely sent to another monastery, Orbais, in northeastern France.

Some years later Gottschalk again ran afoul of church authorities. Inspired by his study of the teachings of Saint Augustine, he had become a proponent of the idea of predestination—a sixth-century doctrine that had fallen out of favor in ecclesiastical circles. In essence, predestination stated that God alone determined whether a person would be good or evil, and only the good were subject to salvation. Gottschalk's writing on the subject infuriated Hrabanus Maurus, his former abbot, who, like the majority of churchmen of his day, believed that salvation from sin was available to everyone through the church.

As a result of Maurus's efforts, Gottschalk in 848 was called before another council of clerics in Mainz. He was charged with heresy and convicted, then flogged until, in the words of an eyewitness, "he was nearly dead." Afterwards, the council ordered that he be kept under lock and key at Orbais to prevent him from contaminating others with his sacrilegious ideas. He remained there until his death in 868.

Though Gottschalk did not live to see it, the kind of academic freedom that he had yearned for eventually became available to monks and laymen alike. Some two hundred years after Gottschalk's death, a man named Peter Abelard was born on the Brittany peninsula in western France. The first-born son of a knight,

his intellectual brilliance outshone many of his contemporaries, but he was even more renowned for his role in one of history's greatest love stories.

Abelard had always been encouraged in his hunger for knowledge by his father who, as Abelard put it, "had tasted little of letters before he became a knight," but "afterwards embraced letters with such love" that he wanted his sons "instructed in letters before they were trained in arms." This was the reverse of a typical nobleman's education, and Abelard's father may have eventually come to regret his decision, for Abelard gave up all rights to his father's knighthood for a lifelong pursuit of intellectual enlightenment. "I preferred the conflict of disputations to the trophies of battle," he wrote, and a more combative disputant would be hard to find. As a brash young knight might have vanquished more seasoned rivals, so Abelard challenged and bested many of his highly esteemed teachers.

While still a young man, Abelard moved to Paris to attend lectures given at the cathedral school by the distinguished educator William of Champeaux. But before long, Abelard had set up his own competing school just outside the Paris city limits, an act he referred to as "laying siege" to William. Glib and witty, Abelard jousted with his former teacher on key elements of philosophy and often won the day. Abandoning William, students flocked to this engaging young lecturer, and Abelard later boasted that his own name grew while the fame of his former teacher was "gradually extinguished."

Abelard next went to the north of France to study with the most famous biblical scholar of his day, Anselm of Laon, who had taught William. But Abelard grew critical of Anselm, and again began giving lectures, based on his own interpretations of the Bible. He drew so many students away that Anselm forbade him to lecture in Laon. Returning to Paris, Abelard became a canon—a clergyman on the staff of a cathedral—and lecturer at the adjacent cathedral school, where his shrewd insights dazzled

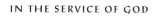

"Here is Hell and the angel who closes the gate," reads the inscription on this 12th-century painting, which depicts the underworld as a monster devouring the souls of the damned.

throngs of enthralled students who came from all over Europe.

A man like Abelard seemed constantly tempted to overreach. In 1119, at the age of 40, he would do so in a manner that would change his life irrevocably. He had thrust all his youthful energies into intellectual pursuits and through the years had remained sexually abstinent. Having attained fame and wealth, he became restless and driven by carnal desires, which he resolved to satisfy by seducing a young woman of his own class.

Characteristically, he took a cool, cerebral approach to the task at hand. First he made an appraisal of his own sex appeal: "So great was my reputation then, and so much did I excel in the grace of youth and beauty, that I feared no rejection from whatever woman I might

would later write that she was distinguished by her "knowledge of letters, rarely found in women. I discerned in her all the things which are likely to attract lovers." And with her delight in learning, Heloise seemed a particularly apt target for his affections, for she would appreciate his own intellectual accomplishments and "would yield to me the more readily."

With the help of mutual friends, he approached her doting uncle and guardian and offered to tutor Heloise, explaining that he needed funds to keep up his household expenses. Fulbert was so eager to advance his niece in her studies, that he agreed that whenever Abelard had time, "whether by day or by night," the scholar could drop by and teach her.

To Abelard, seized with lustful anticipa-

"Under the pretense of study we gave ourselves entirely to love."

favor with my love." He was free to enhance his natural good looks with the grandest fashions of the day, for a canon had no dress code. His finely woven tunic was cut in the latest style, trimmed with bands of embroidery at the neck and hem, sleeves billowing into a bell shape at the wrist; a fur-lined cloak was fixed on one shoulder by a jeweled clasp.

Abelard now searched for a suitable prospect. His eye lit upon the girl next door, Heloise, a 16-year-old whose house adjoined his school at the cathedral. From this short distance, he could study her schoolgirl figure garbed in a floor-length, tight-fitting gown, its V-neck revealing the linen chemise underneath; her waist-length braids spilled out of her hooded mantle. Heloise was the niece of Fulbert, another canon of the Paris cathedral, and had been educated at the nearby convent of Argenteuil. By her midteens she had read the classics. A clearly impressed Abelard

tion, Fulbert's acquiescence was "as if he had committed a tender lamb to a ravenous wolf." Furthermore, Fulbert had assured him that "if I found her negligent, I might harshly punish her." Perhaps threats and blows were needed at the beginning when Heloise, shocked, frightened, and yet attracted to the famous scholar, tried to defend her honor. Before long, however, Heloise was responding with complete abandon to her tutor's caresses, acknowledging years later that "those amorous pleasures that we experienced were so sweet to me" that she still could not get them out of her mind.

The room in Fulbert's house that had been set aside for the tutoring sessions contained a writing desk, book cabinets, and benches. Books were left open and strewn about, for "under the pretense of study we gave ourselves entirely to love," Abelard recalled. "More were the kisses than the learned opinions. No stage

To escape the terrors of hell and achieve eternal salvation, people were instructed to stay close to the church and its teachings. In this 15th-century painting, the congregation kneels respectfully as priests deliver sermons, celebrate Mass, and administer the sacraments.

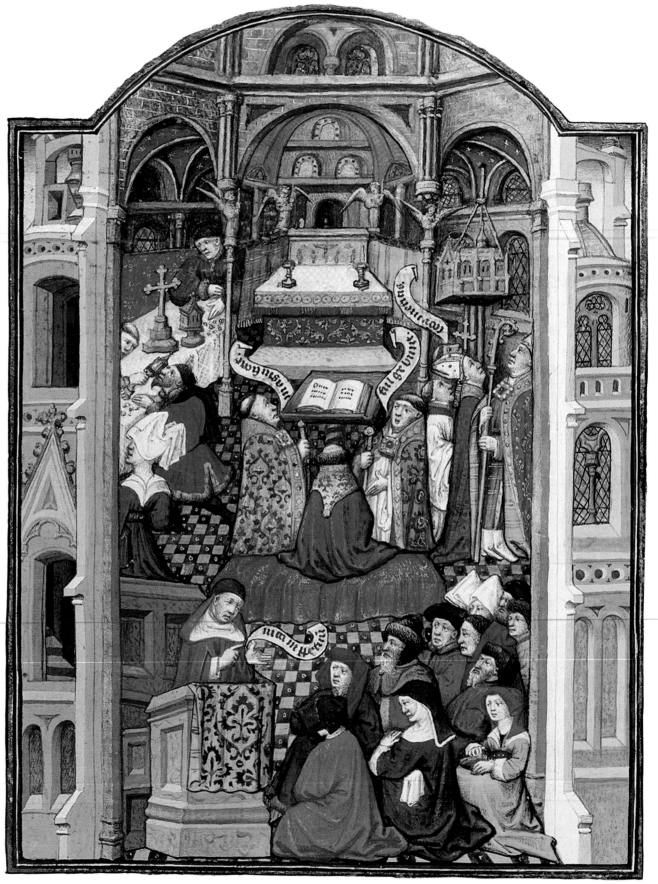

of love escaped our desires. If love could invent some new manner, we tried this too."

Yet despite these delights, all was not going strictly according to plan. Abelard had not foreseen that satisfying his lust would become an all-consuming passion. He later told Heloise, "So intense were the fires of lust, which bound me to you, that I set those wretched, obscene pleasures, which we blush even to name, above God." He became "negligent and indifferent." Unable to concentrate on his lectures, his teaching fell apart. The only accomplishment he was capable of during this time was writing love songs, later incorporated into the repertoires of minstrels.

The affair persisted for many months until his students caught on to what was happening. Only Uncle Fulbert, despite hints from friends, refused to believe it. But one day Fulbert faced the truth, probably after walking in and catching the pair in the act. Outraged, he banned Abelard from his house.

Both lovers found the separation intolerable. Then Heloise discovered that she was pregnant. Ecstatic in the belief that she would now be reunited with Abelard, she wrote to him and together they devised a plan. On a night when her uncle was away from home, Heloise donned a nun's habit, slipped out of Fulbert's house, and journeyed with Abelard to his sister's home in Brittany. There she gave birth to a baby boy to whom she gave the most unusual name Astrolabe, after a scientific instrument used to measure the height of stars from the horizon.

Abelard returned to Paris and assured Fulbert he would wed Heloise. There were married canons and priests at this time, and even a few bishops had wives, but the higher authorities in the church were bent on outlawing the practice. By remaining celibate, they reasoned, a priest set himself on a higher moral plane, removed from the passions and desires that so often plagued his flock. It would take a few decades for this position to become official Catholic policy, but even in Abelard's day, having a wife was seen as a liability. To protect the scholar's reputation, Fulbert agreed to Abelard's request that the nuptials be kept secret.

Neither man had anticipated, however, that Heloise would resist matrimony for Abelard's sake. "How is it fitting," she asked, "for scholars to associate with wet-nurses, to place writing-desks among cradles?" How could he concentrate on his studies amidst "the constant dirty messes of the little ones?" Heloise offered another solution: She would be his mistress, not his wife.

From Heloise's perspective, it made sense. Marriage could be the grave of their great passion, for Abelard would resent being forced into such a burdensome situation. If she

THE POWER OF RELICS

Carried by knights in their sword hilts, worn by pilgrims in small bags around their necks, or displayed in precious gilded or bejeweled reliquaries such as the one below—which contains an arm bone of Saint Babylas, a martyred Syrian bishop—relics were an integral part of religious life in the Middle Ages.

According to the church, remains such as the clothing, bones, or hair of a dead saint were impregnated with the spirit of the deceased, and so possessed mystical properties—the capacity to heal, grant wealth, or confer spiritual blessings.

31

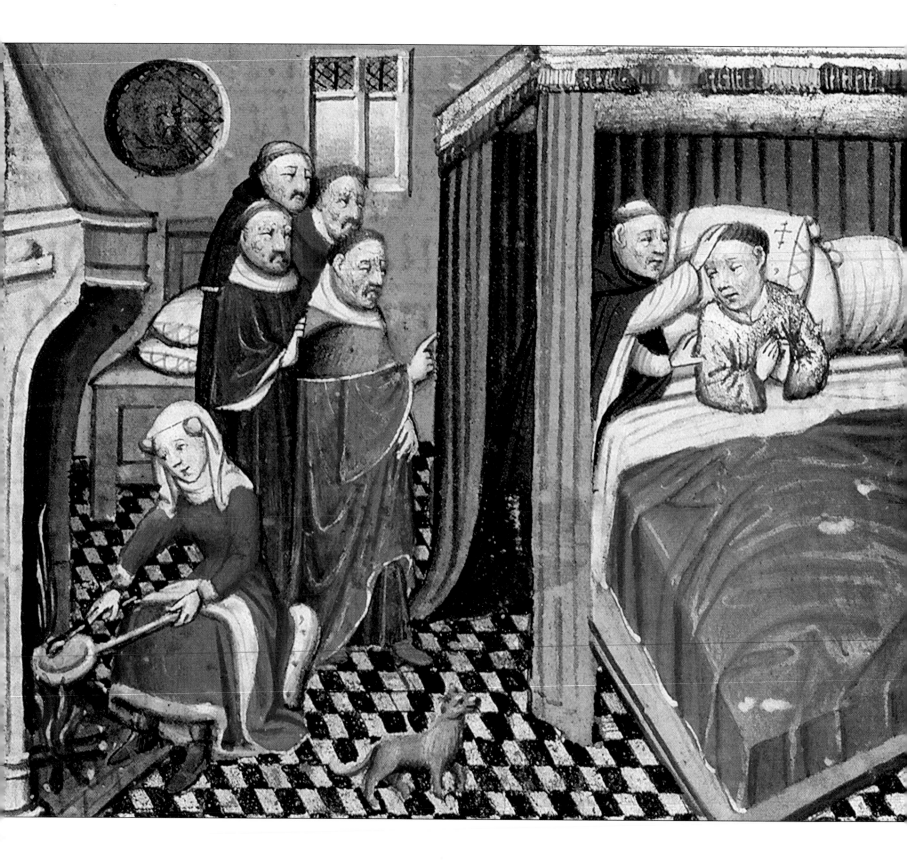

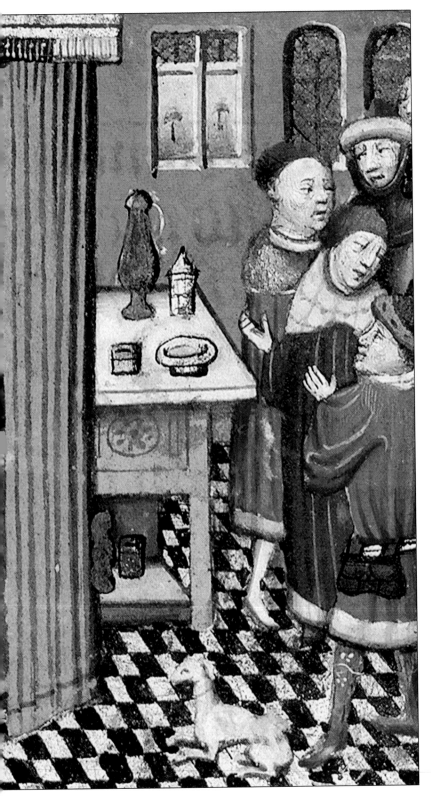

In the presence of both his family and members of the clergy, a dying man receives last rites from a priest.

wanted to keep love alive, it was better to maintain her own establishment and her independence. She continued to assert that she preferred "love to wedlock and freedom to chains." Taking a stance that, for her day, was unprecedented—if not downright scandalous—she argued that free love was morally superior to marriages that all too often were based on the desire for wealth or economic security.

Fearing Fulbert's vengeance, Abelard persuaded Heloise to marry him. The lovers left the baby in the care of Abelard's sister and slipped back into Paris, where they were wed in Fulbert's presence. To keep their nuptials secret, they lived apart. But the secrecy left Fulbert still disgraced, and he began to tell his friends of their wedding. Upon learning this, Abelard packed Heloise off to Argenteuil, the convent where she had received her early schooling. Abelard visited her there at least once, when they made love in a dining hall dedicated to the Blessed Virgin.

When Fulbert learned that Heloise had been sent to a convent, he was convinced that Abelard had abandoned her. He conceived and carried out the cruelest revenge imaginable: After bribing Abelard's servant, Fulbert crept into the scholar's house one night with a few cronies. Finding Abelard asleep in his bedroom, they castrated him and ran off. Two were caught fleeing, and they were in turn castrated and also had their eyes put out. The next morning the story spread throughout the city, leaving the community reeling in shock. Abelard retired to the abbey of Saint-Denis, in a suburb of Paris, and on the same day Heloise took the veil at Argenteuil. But their saga was not yet over.

Seven years before Abelard met Heloise, a 22-year-old man named Bernard, who was destined to play an important role in Peter Abelard's life, was riding with the duke of Burgundy's forces to besiege a castle. One of six well-educated sons of a Burgundian nobleman, the devout young man stopped to pray in a church, where he vowed that he would enter a monastery one

A PILGRIMAGE TO SANTIAGO DE COMPOSTELA

Undertaken as a demonstration of devotion or an act of penance, pilgrimages to holy sites were popular in medieval Europe. One of the favorite destinations—second only to Rome itself—was Spain's Santiago de Compostela, the reputed site of the tomb of the apostle James, known in Spanish as Santiago. To help get there safely, some travelers carried a reference for the journey, the *Pilgrim's Guide*.

The guide described the sights, shrines, and people that pilgrims would encounter. The inhabitants of the province of Poitou, for example, were described as handsome, generous, and good natured, while the Gascons "talk much trivia, are verbose, mocking," and are "badly dressed in rags."

The pilgrimage ended at the cathedral of Santiago. There beneath the high altar lay a marble sarcophagus containing the body of Saint James, which, said the guide, was "decorated with the brightness of celestial candles, and unceasingly honoured by angelic adoration." After touching the sacred reliquary, pilgrims purchased the saint's emblem, a scallop shell *(above)*, before setting out on the long trip home.

Along the way, pilgrims dined at hostels which, noted the *Pilgrim's Guide*, offered "rest to the poor, help to the ill, salvation to the dead."

Saint James *(far left)* was often depicted as a Compostela pilgrim himself, complete with staff, hat with scallop shell, travel bag, and what is probably a leather-bound copy of the Scriptures.

Written in Latin by an unknown Frenchman in the 1130s, the *Pilgrim's Guide* was a prototype of the modern guidebook. A page from the book is shown at left.

The map below indicates the chief pilgrimage routes across France to Santiago de Compostela in northwestern Spain.

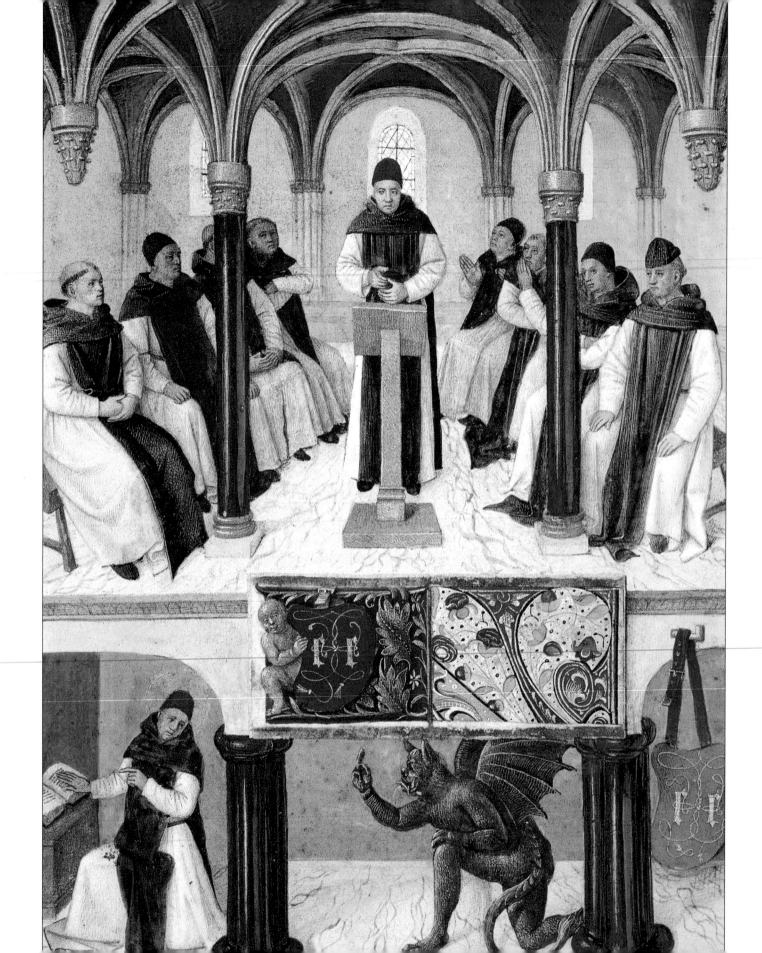

day. Suddenly he heard a voice urging him to bring others into monastic life with him. For months afterward Bernard preached, cajoled, implored, and eventually persuaded many friends and kinsmen to join him. During that same year of 1112, the young knight walked into the monastery of Cîteaux leading a band of 30 men, all clamoring to join the brothers.

A warm, emotional man, Bernard was also an aggressive, relentless proselytizer of converts, possessed of a fiery spirit. Bernard flourished at the monastery, which had recently been reformed and was administered strictly according to the Benedictine Rule. Within three years Bernard was chosen to found a new house at a place called Clairvaux, a desolate, overgrown site near the Aube River, formerly the hideout of a band of thieves. Life was harsh as the monks established their new home, but when the situation seemed hopeless, Bernard would pray and an unexpected donation would appear, as if in

conservative outlook, quite the opposite of Peter Abelard. He rejected an intellectual approach to Christianity, fearing it would leave out the poor and uneducated. He believed that faith alone could bring about a mystical union of the soul with God. Like Abelard, however, he relished the arena of religious debate. Eloquent and polished in his writings and speeches, he was a vigorous champion of his beliefs, yet he was revered for the aura of holiness he projected. A contemporary noted that while his body was "meagre and emaciated, his eyes shone with angelic purity and dovelike simplicity."

Bernard relentlessly criticized those of his brethren who had abandoned the monks' traditionally austere lifestyle. His list of priestly transgressions included chanting prayers without devotion, drunkenness and brawling in the cloister, openly possessing private property, keeping concubines, and fathering children. Nuns, according to Bernard,

"His eyes shone with angelic purity and dovelike simplicity."

answer to his prayer. Indeed, throughout his life, Bernard of Clairvaux would be known as a miracle worker.

The Cistercians, as Bernard's order became known, was among the most influential of the monastic organizations; by 1134 there were 30 Cistercian houses, and there were 350 by the time of Bernard's death, some 164 directly under his authority. In addition, more adults were entering the cloistered life, and the Cistercians pioneered the idea of accepting adults on an equal basis with oblates and others who had grown up in the monastery.

Bernard was a complex man who tried to lead the simplest of lives. He developed a decidedly

were often no better: In some convents nuns were found taking bribes, giggling or quarreling during services, wearing fashionable clothing, having sexual relations with monks and priests, and even performing herbal abortions.

Bernard denounced the monks of the Benedictine Order of Cluny, in particular, for their pursuit of fine clothing, observing that "when you want to buy a cowl you traipse from town to town and trail round the markets," turning "the merchant's premises upside down," and seeking "the most distinctive and therefore costliest article." His own clothes were clean but those of a poor man; under them he wore a shirt made of rough animal hair—secretly, so as not to flaunt his self-torment. He ate

Abbot of the monastery of Clairvaux and leader of the Cistercian reform movement, Saint Bernard preaches to his fellow monks. Although he was the most powerful cleric of his day, Bernard was not immune to temptation *(bottom left.)*

bread softened in water, some broth, and drank little wine. He tried to rid himself of the ability to discriminate tastes, so as not to desire more. Perhaps Bernard could have been a little more forgiving of those clerics who failed to live up to his own lofty standards. After all, many monks and nuns had not chosen for themselves the strict regime of the cloister, having been placed there as children by their parents, and some of them were just not suited to it.

Surprisingly, many of Bernard's admonitions would have met with the approval of Peter Abelard, who at Saint-Denis was chafing at the laxity there. Abelard upbraided his fellow monks, "frequently and vehemently," as he put it, for their devotion to a "wicked way of life." Unlike Bernard, who was lauded for his strictness, Abelard knew that he had made himself "odious to all of them."

In 1130 Bernard was invited to attend the Council of Étampes, where a new pope was to be chosen. Finding the cardinals split between two candidates, Innocent II and Anacletus, Bernard persuaded the French royalty and clergy to join him in supporting Innocent II and traveled throughout Europe campaigning for his choice. Finally, in 1137, Innocent, who had been forced to flee to Pisa, returned to Rome and established his papacy. After this victory, Bernard was a major power in church affairs.

It was probably inevitable, given his stature and his views, that Bernard would eventually cross swords with Peter Abelard. After becoming a monk, Abelard had continued his rational approach to scripture in his writings and lectures. He was

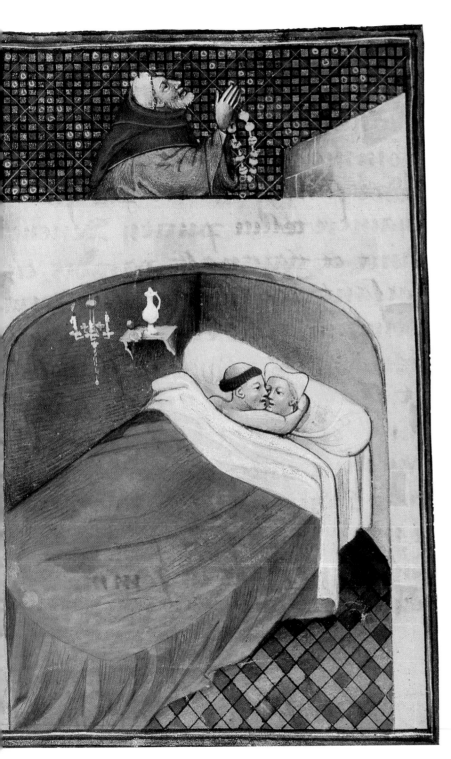

among the first to propose that philosophical reasoning could be a component of faith. Continuing this line of thought, he put forward the radical notion that, since Christian theology was logical, thinking men who had lived before Jesus could have somehow sensed his embodiment of the divine spirit and could benefit from his salvation of the human soul.

In 1121 he was hauled before a council of clerics in Soissons. Without being accorded a chance to defend himself, he was forced to toss his book, *On the Divine Unity and Trinity*, into a fire, under the eyes of his critics. He was then marched across the river, to the jeers of onlookers, and became a prisoner in the local abbey, where he languished awhile before returning to Saint-Denis.

A year later Abelard was granted a parcel of land on which he erected a small mud-and-thatch chapel he called the Paraclete, a name for the Holy Spirit, meaning comforter. Intending to become a hermit, he was soon surrounded by students who had sought him out. In 1125 a duke arranged for Abelard to become an abbot in one of his monasteries in remote Brittany, Saint-Gildas-de-Rhuys, notorious for its laxity. He spent four depressing years trying to reform the monks of Saint-Gildas, some of whom allegedly kept concubines and their children on the side. It was a task fraught with danger, not to mention irony, given Abelard's own past. The brothers were so hostile, Abelard contended, that they had tried to poison him, for when he turned down a dish of food, the monk who ate it died.

It was then that the plight of his former lover, Heloise,

Unscrupulously taking advantage of his position and a couple's hospitality, a monk dines with the pair in one scene of this painting and in the next—while his host is at prayer—commits adultery with the man's wife.

started him on a fresh path with a renewed purpose in life. Heloise at 25 had become prioress—or head nun—at Argenteuil. Her swift rise to leadership attested to her competence in administration as well as her intelligence and education. During their years of separation, Heloise and Abelard had undoubtedly taken a great interest in each other's progress. Now Abelard discovered that Heloise and her nuns were in trouble, and his former monks at Saint-Denis were the cause.

The abbot of Saint-Denis had discovered a claim to the property of Argenteuil. He charged the nuns there with improprieties and insisted that the convent be disbanded and its lands transferred to his abbey. No accusations were made against Heloise herself, nor was she held responsible for the actions of the allegedly wayward sisters.

Upon learning of Heloise's difficulties, Abelard resolved to come to her aid. He sent word to Heloise to meet him at the Paraclete, and then he galloped halfway across France for a rendezvous with his onetime mistress and wife. There they stood, face to face at last, outfitted in the solemn habits of their orders—she, still a young woman in her twenties, he, a weary man of 50, both touched by romantic memories and still experiencing great affection for one another.

Abelard made Heloise a magnanimous offer—the lands of the Paraclete. There she and a select group of her nuns would establish a new convent where Heloise would be abbess, an arrangement that, by 1131, was approved by both the bishop and the pope. Of her administration of the new convent, Abelard was full of praise, "God allowed such grace to fall over that sister of mine, who was over the other nuns, that bishops loved her like a daughter, abbots like a sister, and laymen like a mother."

From the moment the nuns settled in at the Paraclete, Abelard worked tirelessly on their behalf, often visiting Heloise to bring her material that he thought could be useful to the convent, such as collections of hymns, liturgical works, and sermons, including some of his own. In return for his efforts,

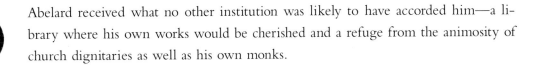

Abelard received what no other institution was likely to have accorded him—a library where his own works would be cherished and a refuge from the animosity of church dignitaries as well as his own monks.

In the last decade of Abelard's life, his work came under assault by Bernard, who wrote his *Treatise against the Errors of Peter Abelard,* and in 1140 accused Abelard of heresy. Abelard spent his last years fighting Bernard's charges, requesting a final decision on the matter from the pope. Before judgment could be rendered, Abelard became terminally ill. Shortly before Abelard died at the age of 63 in 1142, he wrote verses offering moral lessons to his son, Astrolabe, who, by then, had become a priest.

Despite Bernard's criticisms, Abelard triumphed after all; in later years churchmen agreed that Abelard's work had been misrepresented, and Bernard's attacks so extreme as to be unworthy of the saintly monk. The views Bernard had contested, although novel at the time, became mainstream church doctrine.

Heloise maintained her own sterling reputation and that of the Paraclete until her death in 1164. Even Bernard, who visited the Paraclete in 1131, wrote of being welcomed "like an angel," which probably speaks as much to Heloise's prudence as to her hospitality. Yet she was not entirely reconciled to the life of a nun. In letters to Abelard, she revealed a gnawing unhappiness. She wrote of having "denied myself every pleasure in obedience to your will," and called his instruction to take the veil a "command to destroy myself." But she expressed an abiding affection, "You alone have the power to make me sad, to bring me happiness."

His letters, in contrast, are filled with philosophical advice, and the confession that what he had felt for her was lust, not love.

The lasting fame of this couple was based on this correspondence, written during Heloise's first decade at the Paraclete. Chiding, questioning, debating, sometimes recalling their tempestuous affair, they explored their spiritual concerns. And through these letters, their love passed into legend.

Despite his vast achievements as a religious scholar, Peter Abelard is best remembered for his love affair with his student Heloise.

Monastic Life

"Whoever you are, renounce your own will, and take up the strong and bright weapons of obedience," commanded Saint Benedict in his guidelines of conduct for monks, known as the Rule. Throughout the Middle Ages many heeded Benedict's mandate, flocking to the thousands of monasteries, abbeys, and convents that sprang up all over western Europe. Eventually, more than a dozen different monastic orders evolved, many with branches for women as well as men.

To lessen dependence on the outside world, Saint Benedict decreed that "the monastery should be so laid out that everything essential, that is to say water, mills, garden and workshops for the plying of the various crafts, is found within the monastery walls." Under the direction of an abbot (inset, left), the monastery's head, the design of the complex within those walls was made to conform to the regimen of its residents. The church, the spiritual center of the monastery, was always the dominant structure. Other buildings contained large rooms for use as refectories and dormitories to accommodate the monks' communal lifestyle.

Though they lived apart from society, monks and nuns were not social outcasts. In fact, they garnered widespread respect, and the monastic way of life was upheld as the ideal. The religious orders contributed a great deal to the society, opening up large areas for settlement, educating a largely illiterate populace, and attending to those in need.

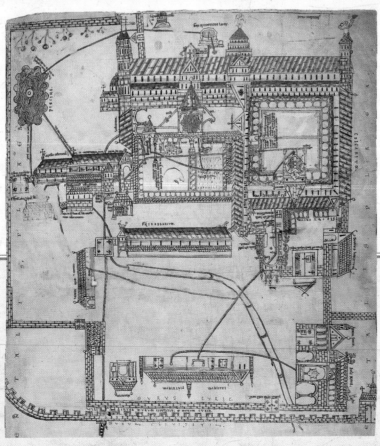

The abbey of Saint Martin-du-Canigou perches atop a cliff in southern France. Its isolation served to keep monks from worldly temptations.

A diagram of the Benedictine abbey of Canterbury illustrates the self-sufficiency of a 12th-century monastery. Water pipes, represented by red lines, led from a reservoir to the kitchen garden (herbarium), the dining hall (refectorium), and to the 55 latrines of the necessarium.

God's Work

Fully half of a monk's waking hours were spent in prayer, known as *opus Dei,* or God's work. Saint Benedict considered communal worship the most important activity of a monk. "As soon as the signal for the the Divine Office shall be heard," he instructed, "each one must lay aside whatever work he may be engaged upon and hasten to it, with all speed, but still with gravity. . . . Nothing . . . shall be put before the Divine Office."

At regular intervals from just after midnight until the next evening, the community passed silently through the covered walkways, or cloisters, that provided shelter in bad weather, and gathered for worship at the church. Here the monks prayed, sang psalms, read the gospel, or attended mass. The liturgy varied depending on the hour, day, and season, but communal worship averaged about five hours a day; four more hours might be spent in private prayer and contemplation.

Through this intense devotion, a monk hoped to overcome the temptations of the flesh and open his mind and soul to God. Though difficult, the contemplative life had its own rewards, both in this life and in the next, said Benedict: "The path of God's commandments is run with unspeakable loving sweetness; so that . . . persevering in the monastery until death . . . , we share by our patience the sufferings of Christ, and so merit to be partakers in His Kingdom."

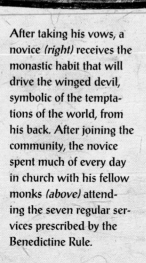

After taking his vows, a novice *(right)* receives the monastic habit that will drive the winged devil, symbolic of the temptations of the world, from his back. After joining the community, the novice spent much of every day in church with his fellow monks *(above)* attending the seven regular services prescribed by the Benedictine Rule.

Graceful columns line the cloister of the abbey of Monreale in Sicily.

Books copied by monks in the scriptorium *(below)* also included classics, such as the works of Virgil and Ovid, and scientific and scholarly tomes. In this way, knowledge that might have been lost was passed on to subsequent generations. Clergymen like Richard of Wallingford *(right)* plotted the liturgical calendar from such texts. Here, he uses a compass and square to make an astrolabe, an instrument for calculating the date and time from the stars' position.

Mind and Body

Every aspect of a monk's life was strictly regulated. The Rule recommended only one meal a day for the brethren, with a cold snack in the evening. Moreover, the meal could be quite austere: "We consider it to be enough for the daily meal . . . that there should always be served two cooked dishes," Benedict declared. Bread was the main staple, supplemented by eggs, cheese, fish, and vegetables.

The monks ate together at assigned places at tables in the refectory. Talking was prohibited, so the brothers developed an elaborate system of sign language. At least 100 recorded signals, such as reaching for the throat as a request for vinegar, were used by the monks. While the brothers ate, one of their members, known as a lector, read from the Scriptures or a devotional work, to ensure that mealtime fed the spirit as well as the body.

After the meal the monks spent some time reading and interpreting the Scriptures and other religious literature. Books of the period were handwritten on parchment, and so were both expensive and scarce. To increase the size of a monastery's library, the abbot put monks to work copying manuscripts, and a special room, the scriptorium, was set aside for this purpose. The copying of texts not only helped to preserve classical literature but also provided educational materials that could be used in monastery schools. Benedict considered copying to be of great spiritual benefit, saying, "Every word that you write is a blow that smites the devil."

A nun reads aloud at the daily meal *(left)*; a medieval lector's pulpit (holding an organ) overlooks the large refectory of France's Royaumont monastery *(right)*.

To Work Is to Pray

On entering a monastery, novices were often reminded of the dictum *laborare est orare*, that is, to work is to pray. According to the Rule, monks were to spend at least three hours a day performing manual labor. This meant that every waking hour not spent in worship or study was to be spent working. In this way, each day would be filled with activity and would prevent the occurrence of idleness, which Benedict labeled "the enemy of the soul."

Before long, however, many monasteries relaxed this requirement. Frequent church services precluded putting in a good day's work in the fields, and the monks, who often were of noble birth, preferred to let others dirty their hands. Instead, peasants took over much of the agricultural work on monastic lands, and lay brothers and servants functioned as cooks, bakers, barbers, and tailors. By the late 11th century, the reform-minded Cistercian order reintroduced the concept of hard work into the monastic routine, asserting that "food for monks of our order ought to come from manual labour, agriculture, and the raising of animals." But for most monks, less-taxing chores, like brewing beer and mending clothes, made up the bulk of their daily labors.

The kitchen garden of Fontevrault monastery in France still supplies the monks' table.

Monks plow and till the soil of their abbey's land while their fellow workers break for refreshment *(above)*. A monastery's self-sufficiency could extend to the provision of all food and drink for the monks. The job of the cellarer *(above, right)* included holding the keys to the monastery's precious stores of food and drink and testing its wines. Almost every monastery brewed its own beer *(right)*, to be imbibed, in limited quantities, along with meals.

CHAPTER TWO

Loyal Men and True

Using scaling ladders and bombards for hurling stones, English soldiers attack the French at the siege of Brest during the Hundred Years' War. Siege warfare, an important part of medieval military operations, involved prolonged battles in which armies attempted to breach the fortifications of their opponents who, cut off from supplies, slowly starved.

part from the boy in the catapult basket, it was just another battle—a minor flareup in the long-running civil war between King Stephen, struggling to hold on to the throne of England, and his challenger, Queen Matilda, the daughter of Henry I. A band of men loyal to Stephen had laid siege to a castle at Newbury, just west of London. Queen Matilda's forces, led by a crusty gent named John Marshal, stood fast within the stronghold.

By this stage of the conflict—the year was 1152—the combatants on both sides of the lines had seen a bit too much of fighting. They were grateful, then, when John Marshal sent out a message calling for a one-day truce. If King Stephen would grant the respite, Marshal promised, he would attempt to persuade Queen Matilda to surrender the castle. Suspecting trickery, the king agreed only if Marshal would offer a guarantee in the form of a hostage—his youngest son, William. John Marshal did not even hesitate; the five-year-old boy was duly sent into the enemy camp as security against his father's pledge.

But John Marshal had no intention of keeping his word. Instead, he took advantage of the break in action to bring in more provisions and fresh troops. Stephen was outraged and let it be known that he would not take the affront lightly. The young boy, William, would be slaughtered at the very gates of the castle.

A messenger brought this grim news from the king and waited to hear John Marshal's response. If Stephen expected his foe to yield, he hadn't reckoned on Marshal's iron resolve. Earlier in the war, while bottled up in an abandoned church, Marshal had refused to submit even when Stephen's men set the church roof ablaze, showering him with molten lead. Marshal lost an eye, but stood his ground.

Now, with his young son's life hanging in the balance, Marshal's battle-scarred face betrayed no emotion. The king could do what he liked with the boy, said the defiant warrior. After all, he boasted, he still had "the hammer and the forge to produce another such, even finer."

Marshal's answer only stiffened the king's resolution. A large siege catapult rolled up to the battle lines. Its weighted firing beam had the power to hurl a 150-pound boulder some 200 yards, smashing through the stone walls of all but the sturdiest castle. On this fateful day, however, the king's men had placed young William Marshal into the catapult's load basket. The boy appeared to find the entire spectacle greatly amusing. He cheerfully called out over his shoulder, wanting to know what sort of game the men were playing.

Examples of medieval finery adorn the carved wooden statues of, left to right, John IV of Brabant, Jacoba of Hainault, Albert of Bavaria, Philip the Good, and Mary of Burgundy. The statues, which grace the tomb of Isabella of Bourbon, portray her illustrious relatives.

But in the end, Stephen had no stomach for the murder of an innocent boy; John Marshal had called the king's bluff—and won. Stephen withdrew his forces from Newbury, keeping William as a forfeit for his father's treachery. The boy was too young to be of use in the royal household, but the king kept him close by anyway, even condescending on occasion to play a game of "straw knights" with his young captive. John Marshal, meanwhile, renewed his campaign in the service of Queen Matilda. If he thought of young William, he very likely felt a sense of resignation at his fate. In any case, he did not see his son again until the war's end four years later, when Stephen returned William to his family.

It would be unfair to say that men of John Marshal's time were indifferent to the welfare of their sons; one chronicle tells of a father who, seeing his son dangled over the edge of a tower, gave in to his foe's demand and castrated himself rather than watch the boy dropped to his death. But Marshal belonged to a class of men who ranked stoicism uppermost in the catalog of manly virtues. For him, the proper response to a crisis was a steely fortitude.

A certain degree of imperturbability was necessary to survive in a world of shifting loyalties and back-room intrigue. The royal courts of Europe were hotbeds of rumor and backstabbing. Dukes, barons, and lesser nobles took every advantage of the general chaos to increase their power through outright thievery.

In these dangerous times, kings and barons alike strengthened their households with bands of soldiers who offered protection in return for pay or, in some cases, plunder. These men were equipped at their lord's ex-pense with armor and trappings bearing his crest and colors. In time they came to be known as knights, and their high morale, military ritual, and rigid code of behavior became the stuff of legend. By the end of the 12th century, knights in armor would come to exemplify a sense of honor and duty known as chivalry—from the French word *chevalarie,* which literally means "what the horse soldiers did." But these soul-stirring days still lay ahead during King Stephen's reign, and in a sense, much of the bloodshed and misery of his rule can be traced to a single incident that occurred in the year 1120.

At that time Britain was enjoying a period of peace and stability under Stephen's uncle, King Henry I. In fact, the country had been mostly calm since 1066, when Henry's father, William the Conqueror, had come to power. And as Henry now entered his old age, the stage was set for a peaceful transition of power to his son, William.

Then, with one tragic misfortune, Henry's careful plans blew apart. He and his royal household were crossing the English Channel from Normandy, as they had done many times before. The king traveled in his own ship and landed safely in England. William had crowded onto a vessel called the *White Ship*, said to be the proudest in all the royal fleet, along with most of the other members of Henry's court. Without the restraining presence of the king, the royal household apparently decided to take advantage of the fine weather and make a party of it. The crew broke out casks of wine and spirits, and general merriment carried the day—so much so that no one noticed as the ship sailed into a jagged rock and tore open its wooden hull. The *White Ship* went down without a trace, taking with it the heir to the

throne and all the rest of the passengers and crew except for one butcher, who straggled ashore half-drowned to tell the tale.

In an instant, Henry I's plans were undone. All of his hopes for a peaceful succession had rested on the shoulders of William, his only son. The king fainted away when told of the disaster, and it was said that he never smiled again.

An aging widower, Henry did what he could to salvage his bloodline. He attempted to have another son by a new wife, without success. Then, when his daughter Matilda, who had been married off to German royalty, suddenly became a widow, Henry leapt at the opportunity. He insisted that Matilda return to

French soldiers *(shown on left in battlefield)*, many heavily armored, begin their retreat at the Battle of Crécy as the English army advances on them. The English, whose longbows and strategic planning represented a revolution in warfare and brought them an overwhelming victory, lost only a hundred men to France's 1,500.

England and marry Geoffrey, the 15-year-old son of the powerful count of Anjou. The marriage was not an especially happy one, but it brought about the desired result: In 1133 King Henry was presented with a grandson, also named Henry.

Had the king lived another 10 years or so, England might have been spared a great deal of suffering. Unhappily, when his grandson was only two years old, Henry sat down to a meal of lamprey eels—"though they never agreed with him"—and died of acute indigestion.

A feud over the royal succession was inevitable. On one side were the forces loyal to Matilda and her two-year-old son, who had the strongest claim to the throne. But many of England's powerful nobles had little taste for a female monarch, especially one who had spent most of her life in Germany. Even before Henry I's untimely death, Matilda's haughty behavior had opened the door to a challenge from Stephen of Blois, a favorite nephew of the late king.

After a few minor skirmishes, the anxious nation threw its support to Stephen. He was crowned at Westminster Abbey scarcely three weeks after the death of Henry I. For 19 years Britain staggered under Stephen's weak rule. "Every rich man built him castles and held them against the king," wrote a horrified chronicler. "They cruelly oppressed the wretched people of the country with forced labor on the castles; and when the castles were built, they filled them with devils and evil men. Then took they those whom they supposed to have any goods, both by night and by day, laboring men and women, and threw them into prison for their gold and silver, and inflicted on them unutterable tortures . . . I neither can, nor may I tell all the wounds and all the pains which they inflicted on wretched men in this land. This lasted the nineteen winters while Stephen was king, and it grew continually worse and worse."

While this cloud of gloom settled over England, Matilda's son, Henry, matured and formed his own plans to take back the throne. As the duke of Normandy, Henry had a strong base of power to draw upon. Even so, Stephen wasn't terribly worried. Henry had made an earlier attempt, at the age of 14, to recapture the crown, and the foray had ended so badly that the teenager had to appeal to Stephen himself for money to return to Normandy. So when the slightly older and wiser Henry crossed to Britain and began negotiating with a powerful earl for his support, Stephen barely lifted an eyebrow. He simply bought off the troublesome earl with a generous grant of land. Once again, Henry went back to Normandy empty-handed.

Henry's fortunes were shortly to receive a powerful boost in the form of Queen Eleanor of Aquitaine, the wife of France's King Louis VII. The precarious state of the French royal marriage had been a source of distress throughout Europe, with the pope himself attempting to play Cupid by encouraging the couple to share quarters on a visit to the papal court.

Sadly, the pope's efforts had little effect, and in March of 1152 the royal marriage was dissolved. Eleanor instantly became Europe's most eligible female, with all the qualities designed to attract ambitious young nobles—beauty, intelligence, and an enormous amount of land. Her ancestral property, the Aquitaine, covered all of southwestern France from the Loire Valley to the Pyrenees. All across Britain and France, ardent young suitors rushed to press their attentions on her—forcibly, in some cases—making her journey from her former husband's court precarious. Near the town of Tours, Eleanor was ambushed by 18-year-old Geoffrey of Anjou, Henry's younger brother, who apparently planned to take her for his own. Eleanor's escorts managed to fend off his advances, and the convoy made its way to a crossing of the Loire.

Safely in her own lands, Eleanor decided it would be prudent to select an appropriate second husband for herself. Her attentions quickly fastened on young Henry. She was said to have been much impressed with a glimpse of the duke she caught some time earlier, thundering across a field on a foaming stallion, with a falcon perched on his wrist and a jaunty flower stuck in his cap.

Eleanor sent word to Henry that she was willing to become his wife, bringing the entire duchy of Aquitaine with her by way of a dowry. Henry rushed to accept and on May 18, less than two months after the annulment of her marriage to Louis, the duke of Normandy and the duchess of Aquitaine were married.

Though Eleanor was 11 years older than Henry, the marriage started off well. Both had much to gain from the union. Eleanor had hitched her fortunes to a rising young power and was now safe from unwanted suitors. For Henry the marriage brought a great expansion of his already formidable power base in France. Although technically a vassal of King Louis, Henry now actually controlled more of France than the king did.

Bolstered by his new strength, Henry rallied his supporters and crossed over to England once more in 1153, this time presenting himself with the authority and confidence of a king. The position of King Stephen, meanwhile, had grown much weaker. England's powerful barons had become disenchanted, in part due to Stephen's shabby treatment of church officials. At one stage the bishop of Salisbury had been imprisoned in a cowshed, while the archbishop of Canterbury, denied permission to attend a church council in France, was obliged to slip across the Channel in a dilapidated boat with his faithful household clerk, one Thomas Becket.

Though Stephen and Henry both raised armies for their looming conflict, neither man appeared enthusiastic for battle. Their forces met at Malmesbury, but Stephen quickly pulled back and left the town and its castle to his young challenger.

Henry had time on his side. With every passing month more barons defected to his side, while the older nobles who opposed his claims were dying off. The final blow to Stephen's reign came when his son Eustace died unexpectedly, leaving his father without a successor. A deal was struck: So long as his extensive estates would pass to his heirs, Stephen agreed to recognize Henry as his successor. As it turned out, Henry did not have long to wait. Stephen died the following year.

Henry's coronation on December 19, 1154, proved a hasty, somewhat bedraggled affair. Westminster Abbey, the traditional site for the consecration of English kings, had

The tomb effigies of King Henry II of England and his wife, Eleanor of Aquitaine, in Fontevrault-l'Abbaye, France, lie in serene repose, a marked contrast to their tumultuous life together.

fallen into disrepair during Stephen's tumultuous reign. Against this rather dingy backdrop, Henry's youth and vigor appeared all the more striking to the people of London, who were greatly reassured by his royal demeanor. "In London," recorded one witness, "the young king was received with transports of joy."

The newly crowned Henry II was only 21 years of age. Broad shouldered and barrel chested, the red-haired, freckled Henry looked more like a countryman than a king. Matters of appearance and dress did not greatly concern him, but his natural charm and lack of pretense more than compensated. Henry, a courtier observed, was "a man blest with soundness of body and charm of countenance, and one whom people, having looked at carefully a thousand times, would yet run to look upon."

Despite his rough-hewn appearance, Henry was a man of deep learning, fluent in many languages, who enjoyed debating with the clerks of his court and any scholars who happened to cross his path. On the whole he displayed a gentle spirit, but when his temper showed through it was terrible to behold. Once, when a courtier spoke well of one of Henry's rivals, the king flew into a frenzy and reportedly tore the covers from his bed and began to gnaw the straw mattress.

At his leisure, the king loved to hunt in the vast royal forests. He particularly enjoyed hawking—in which trained falcons and hawks were used to bring down birds that had flown beyond the range of arrows. Henry often traveled with a favorite bird perched on a leather glove, and he and his nobles would bring them to the banquet table to partake of any spare morsels. Though at one point the royal forests covered fully a third of the country, Henry did not take kindly to trespassers on his hunting preserves: Poachers were hanged or mutilated. A later decree stated that anyone who found a lost falcon and failed to return it would be punished severely; the bird would be allowed to eat six ounces of flesh from the culprit's breast.

For all of that, Henry was no tyrant. "I once crossed the Channel with him with twenty-five ships which were placed at his service for the crossing without charge," recalled one courtier. "A storm, however, scattered the ships and drove them all upon the rocks and shores ill-suited for ships, except his alone, which, by God's grace, was brought safely to port. He sent out in the morning, therefore, and, learning from each sailor the estimated amount of his loss, he reimbursed him, although he was not bound to do this, and the entire sum amounted to a good deal." "Perchance," the courtier concluded with wry understatement, "there are some kings who do not pay their just debts."

England thrived under Henry II's rule—so much so that the enduring phrase "Merrie England" was coined to capture the general mood. In his early years much of Henry's prodigious energy was spent reversing the effects of the previous 19 years of Stephen's reign. He destroyed or seized some 1,000 unauthorized castles from potentially troublesome nobles and he reasserted English claims to power in Wales and Scotland.

Much of the credit for Henry's early successes must go to his counselors, and most particularly to his chancellor, Thomas Becket, the former clerk of the archbishop of Canterbury. Becket's poise and intelligence made him stand out among the usual crowd of underlings that made up a king's court. The son of a merchant, Becket had raised himself up through dogged hard work, at one time toiling away as a bookkeeper.

Perhaps owing to his humble origins, Becket had a genuine love for the pomp and splendor of court life. Soon the chancellor's establishment in London became the model of courtly cus-

tom—much to the chagrin of Queen Eleanor, who, unlike her low-key husband, also had a taste for the high life. At that time it was common practice for noblemen to send their sons to be raised in a great man's household, the better to be schooled in refined conduct. As Becket's reputation grew, more barons sent their sons to him than to the king. Indeed, one of Henry's own sons was raised in the more rarefied air of Becket's residence.

Becket's lavish hospitality showed itself most particularly at his feasting table. The setting was grand—a large banquet hall with high, wood-beamed ceilings—but the food itself was hit-or-miss. Servants hurried as they carried the heavy platters across a large open court from the kitchen, genuflecting as they approached the table, but the distance between oven and table guaranteed that the food arrived lukewarm, and perhaps even wet with rain. The meat tended to be tough and stringy, but there was plenty of it: starlings, gulls, herons, storks, and vultures all found their way to the banquet table. Larger animals were cut up and cooked immediately upon killing, or heavily salted and soaked in brine for preservation. Spices—especially pepper, mustard, and garlic—were used liberally in the kitchen and at the table. Vegetables were frowned upon as commoners' food, and medical opinion counseled against eating raw fruit.

If the quality of the food was inconsistent, the presentation was spectacular. On any given night Becket's table might feature a roasted peacock with its tail feathers in full display, or a cooked swan gliding across a pond of green pastry, or a meat pie that released a cloud of small birds when cut open—providing target practice for the nobles' falcons. If the cooks were feeling mischievous, they might sew the head and forequarters of a piglet onto the body of a rooster. For dessert, sculptures of paste, jelly, and sug-

Hunting horns like the one above, made of brass and leather, were used to signal dogs and hunters. Below, the call goes out during the chase as the hunting party closes in on its prey.

ar—called subtleties—offered even more latitude to the cooks' creative impulses as they fashioned likenesses of heroes and saints. Becket could not have known that in a few years' time, countless subtleties would be created in his own image.

Various "Bokes of Curtesye" laid out the table manners expected of a polite dinner guest. A gentleman was permitted to pick out tasty morsels with his fingers and offer them to his companion, but he was discouraged from buttering bread with his thumb, poking his finger into eggs, or wiping his teeth on the tablecloth.

While such things mattered a great deal to Becket, King Henry was rather more careless about his table. One guest commented rather snippily on the "half-baked bread" and "stale fish and meat" that was offered in Henry's household. "The wine is turned sour or mouldy—thick, greasy, stale, flat and smacking of pitch. I have sometimes seen even great lords served with wine so muddy that a man

Situated in the middle of a natural lake, Belgium's Beersel Castle was virtually unassailable.

A MAN'S HOME...

Throughout the Middle Ages, Europe's rulers built strongholds along the frontiers of their realms to guard against the constant threat of invasion. The earliest castles were simple earth-and-timber forts located along trade routes or likely avenues of attack. As kingdoms grew in power and wealth, these forts were replaced by massive permanent structures with thick stone walls.

The first requirement for a castle was that it be difficult to reach, and the easiest way to do this was to build in a naturally inaccessible location. William Marshal's Chepstow Castle, for example, rises from a cliff on the Wye River in Wales, leaving attackers few lanes of approach. Others were built on islands or steep hill-

tops. Where there was no natural defense, builders created one by digging a moat around the castle. Some moats were filled with water diverted from a nearby river, but most were not, as even a dry moat presented a formidable obstacle. The only access over the moat was a bridge, which could be drawn into the castle. Large gatehouses guarded entry to the bridge.

The castles themselves boasted ingenious defenses. The battlements, which give castle walls their familiar notched silhouette, afforded shelter as

Caen Castle's drawbridge, which hung from the two protruding beams, was destroyed long ago *(near right)*. A parapet at Beersel Castle *(far right)* has openings for dropping stones and shooting arrows. If the walls were breached, defenders could slide down the chute at center into the lake.

archers returned fire through "arrow slits" cut into them. Many battlements were also built with overhangs called machicolations. These had holes in the floors so the defenders could drop stones or hot oil on any invaders who reached the castle walls. If an enemy did manage to get inside the castle, he would have to dodge stones dropped through "murder holes" cut in the ceilings. In their castle at Ghent, Belgium, the counts of Flanders went so far as to put murder holes in the floor of the second-story chapel.

Though castles were first and foremost defensive structures, they also served as residences for the lord and his family. Inside, elaborate vaults and buttresses created soaring interiors that were often as elegant as they were strong. A castle had to house not only its master—in as grand style as possible—but also a garrison of soldiers and the retinue of servants required to keep it running. To meet the huge demand for services and supplies, entire towns often sprang up around a castle—a fact sometimes reflected in the town's name, like Newcastle upon Tyne in England.

KEEPING CLEAN
The plumbing systems of medieval castles were remarkably sophisticated. A cistern on the top floor provided running water, which fed sinks throughout the castle. Toilets were usually built jutting out of an exterior wall, like the narrow one in the above photo of Haut Koenigsburg Castle in Germany. Waste fell through a hole in the floor either into a pit that was periodically flushed out or directly into a river or lake.

The kitchen at Eltz Castle in Germany contains a large central oven. Many castles had their kitchens in a separate building to reduce the risk of fire.

must needs close his eyes and clench his teeth, wry-mouthed and shuddering, and filtering the stuff rather than drinking."

Far from begrudging Becket his more brilliant court and luxurious table, Henry often dropped by unannounced because he so enjoyed his chancellor's company. Though Becket was older by 15 years, the two men became close companions and could often be found hunting together. Henry valued the older man's integrity and even found amusement in a streak of prudishness that showed itself when the king's revels tested the limits of decorum. Over-indulgence in wine was not unknown in Henry's day, nor did the charms of certain attractive ladies pass unnoticed. At such times Becket quietly withdrew, leaving his sovereign shaking his head in amusement.

In April of 1162, upon the death of the archbishop of Canterbury, Henry named Becket to the office. To the king, it seemed an ideal appointment. Becket

A bedroom at Eltz Castle still contains the enclosed berth in which one of the masters of the household slept. Attendants often slept in the same room.

Castle life was centered around a great hall, like that of England's Hedingham Castle *(left)*. Here, the lord both took his meals and conducted his business.

While musicians entertain, a stream of servants carry in an elaborate evening's feast for the enjoyment of the hosts, their guests, and the dogs of the house.

would continue to serve as chancellor but would also be in a position to smooth over Henry's prickly relations with the church. Henry was struggling to lay the foundations of an equitable judicial system, but these efforts brought him into conflict with the church, which had its own courts. Criminals of all stripes soon learned that by claiming "benefit of clergy," they could plead their cases before the more lenient church courts. Benefit of clergy could be established simply by quoting a few lines of Latin or Bible verses, which became known as "neck verses." It is some indication of the abuse of this privilege that during the early years of Henry's reign no fewer than 100 murders were committed by so-called "clerks of the church."

At first Becket protested that he had no wish to be an archbishop. He had already been branded an enemy of the church by levying punitive taxes; the bishops of the realm were not likely to welcome him as their spiritual leader. Becket probably also understood, though Henry did not, that his new role would inevitably create friction with his king. Once the new role had been thrust upon him, however, Becket embraced it with uncommon fervor. He cast aside the pleasures and luxuries of court life for the more modest habits of a cleric. In the belief that self-punishment purged the soul, Becket put on a coarse, uncomfortable hair shirt and flogged himself daily. He spent long hours in meditation and dedicated himself to the study of the Scriptures.

Henry viewed these changes with alarm, and his concern only deepened when Becket resigned the office of

chancellor. The situation reached its crisis in 1164 when Henry issued a proclamation called the Constitutions of Clarendon, which diminished the independence the church had gained under Stephen. Becket, after initially signing the document, abruptly changed his mind and repudiated it—and punished himself severely for having briefly assented. Henry responded by depriving the archbishop of several castles and estates that Becket still owned from his days as chancellor. Shortly afterward, the king withdrew his son from Becket's household.

At one point Henry attempted to make peace. Meeting in an open field where the two men could talk quietly, Henry pleaded with his old friend, "Have I not raised you from the poor and humble to the pinnacle of honour and rank? You are now not

A French couple contemplate their next moves in a friendly game of chess. Noble lords and ladies whiled away many leisure hours playing the popular game.

only ungrateful but oppose me at every turn." Becket was gracious in his reply, but left little room for compromise, "We ought to obey God, rather than men."

Henry now decided to play rough. He demanded a full accounting of all the money Becket had handled as chancellor of the realm. This was something of a low blow; Becket's dealings as chancellor had generally profited the king far more than Becket himself, and on occasion Becket had even dipped into his own pocket on Henry's behalf. Moreover, upon his consecration as archbishop Becket had received a release from all secular claims that might arise about his years as chancellor. But Henry brushed these points aside, along with Becket's offer of two thousand marks to settle any possible deficiencies. When Becket failed to answer a summons to appear before a royal council at Northampton, Henry charged him with contempt of the king's court.

This was a harsh and perhaps melodramatic reaction by the king, but Becket managed to top it: He presented himself at a clamorous session of the royal council bearing his heavy cross before him like a heavenly shield. By suggesting that he required such divine protection, Becket risked a grave affront to the king—so great, in fact, that his bishops had attempted to wrestle the cross away from him before he entered the council hall. "If the king were to brandish his sword as you now brandish yours," said Gilbert Foliot, the bishop of London, "what hope can there be at making peace between you?" But Becket would not be dissuaded.

The king was not amused by this display. In the end, however, after tense negotiations between his barons and Becket's clerics, Henry satisfied his wounded pride by citing the archbishop to Rome. Becket would not even listen to this verdict. "Think you to judge me?" he demanded. "I will not hear your judgment." With that, he pushed his way out of the chamber, still bearing his cross before him, while boisterous cries of "traitor" echoed behind him.

Knowing Henry's temper as he did, the archbishop wisely decided to remove himself from England. He spent three weeks hiding from Henry's agents before slipping across the English Channel to Flanders. Henry, meanwhile, had seized lands and possessions from Becket's clerks who had aided his flight.

Becket eventually found refuge in an abbey in Burgundy, where he launched a feverish correspondence with nearly every person of influence in Europe, hoping to find supporters. Far from softening his position, the exiled archbishop stepped up his attack, eventually excommunicating the church officials who had endorsed the Constitutions of Clarendon and even threatening Henry himself with a formal church condemnation. But Pope Alexander III hurriedly rescinded Becket's sentences.

Several years passed without any resolution to the feud. Henry became absorbed with problems at home. Though his marriage to Eleanor had produced eight children, the queen tired of Henry's company and withdrew to her own lands in Poitiers. His sons, meanwhile, grew dissatisfied with the limited wealth and influence Henry granted them. In June of 1170, in an effort to keep the peace with his restive heirs, the king arranged the coronation of his 15-year-old son—also named Henry—at Westminster Abbey. No shred of authority passed into the hands of young Henry, who was henceforth known as the Young King, and the lavish ceremony only sharpened the edge of his ambition.

Worse, the coronation fanned the flames of Henry's quarrel with Becket, since the crowning of a king was traditionally the privilege of the archbishop of Canterbury. With Becket in exile, the honor fell to the archbishop of York. The resulting uproar weakened Henry's position and opened the door to a reconciliation with Becket.

A month later the two men met again in a quiet field, away from the castles and courts where their drama had played out. Henry appeared pleased to see his old friend once again, and even sprang from his horse to help Becket with his saddle.

"Come, my Archbishop," the king implored, "let us renew our ancient love for one another; let us show each other all the good we can and forget our old quarrel." All appeared well, and Henry even shed a few tears of joy over the happy meeting, but their reconciliation was short lived.

On Christmas Day, from the pulpit at Canterbury, Becket excommunicated the bishops who had participated in the Young King's coronation. Henry flew into a wild rage when the news reached him. In frustration, he lashed out at the seemingly inept courtiers who surrounded him, "What a parcel of fools and dastards have I nourished in my house, that none of them can be found to avenge me on this one upstart clerk!"

This ambiguous remark, spoken in a moment of fury, sealed the fate of Thomas Becket. That same day, four of the king's knights—described as "hotheaded and in the flower of their age"—slipped away and headed for Canterbury. They found Becket hearing vespers in the cathedral. Uncertain of what to do, and perhaps drunk, the young knights expected the archbishop to cower before them. Instead, it appears they were offered dinner. In their confusion, one of the knights struck Becket on the shoulder with the flat of his sword. "Fly," the young attacker shouted, "you are a dead man!" Becket calmly faced his challengers and bade them do their worst, resisting only when they attempted to drag him from the cathedral. In the struggle, Becket received a blow to the head. Once the archbishop's blood was flowing, the warrior instincts of the four knights took over. They rushed forward and hacked him to death with their swords.

Becket's death shocked Europe. Most horrified of all was Henry, who was painfully aware that his angry remark had inspired the crime. The king threw off his royal robes and dressed himself in the coarse material known as sackcloth and poured ashes over his head as a sign of his sorrow and repentance. Henry's household feared for his life as he withdrew to a private chamber and denied himself food and rest for several days. When he emerged, he felt obliged to go to Ireland until the furor abated.

He lingered in Ireland for six months, then presented himself in France to be purged of his guilt—by means of flogging—and receive absolution. Though his whipping seemed to satisfy the church, Henry made his own peace with Becket on a pilgrimage to Canterbury the following year. "As soon as he was in sight of the church in which the body of the blessed martyr lay buried," wrote a witness to the king's visit, "he dismounted from the horse on which he rode, took off his shoes, and, barefoot, and clad in woolen garments, walked three miles to the tomb of the martyr, with such humility and compunction of heart, that it may be believed beyond a doubt to have been the work of Him who looketh down on the earth, and maketh it to tremble. To those who beheld them, his footsteps, along the road on which he walked, seemed to be covered with blood, and really were so; for his tender feet being cut by the hard stones, a great quantity of blood flowed from them on to the ground. When he had arrived at the tomb, it was a holy thing to see the affliction which he suffered, with sobs and tears, and the discipline to which he submitted from the hands of the bishops and a great number of priests and monks."

While Becket would be canonized within three years, Henry, in a sense, would never recover from the unhappy episode. In time his family would be torn apart by civil war, with Eleanor taking her sons' side against their father. Henry, who once described his heirs as four eaglets bent on his destruction, would see two of them cut down in their prime. Geoffrey, the next-to-youngest son, died after a fall from a horse, while Henry, the Young King, succumbed to a fatal attack of dysentery while leading a campaign against his father.

One of Henry II's knights plunges a sword into the back of Thomas Becket as the archbishop kneels at the altar in Canterbury Cathedral. Declaring himself "ready to die for my Lord," Becket was hacked to pieces in the cathedral's transept.

No sooner had young Geoffrey been buried than Richard, the second of the four sons, renewed the campaign against his father in collusion with King Philip of France. But the 56-year-old Henry had no stomach for more fighting. The bitter and exhausted monarch reached a shaky compromise with Richard and agreed to grant amnesty to all who had participated in the rebellion. Ill and dispirited, Henry had to be borne away from the negotiations on a stretcher.

Sick as he was, he asked his attendant to read out the list of nobles to whom he had promised amnesty. The attendant consulted the list, then hesitated, as if afraid to continue. "Our Lord Jesus Christ help me, Sire," he cried, "the first name written here is that of Count John, your son." This was too much for Henry. John had been his favorite son, the one he believed had remained loyal when his wife and other children turned against him. "Say no more," said the king, turning his face to the wall. Within a few hours he was dead.

One of the last loyal retainers who attended the king on his deathbed and conducted his body to its final resting place was a young man named William Marshal—the very same William Marshal who, years earli-

Such qualities needed to be taught, so William's father had sent him to France to be placed in the home of William de Tancarville, the chamberlain of Normandy, and schooled as a *gentilhomme*. Tancarville was renowned as "the father of knights," and under his care William was to learn the manly arts of horsemanship and combat, as well as the more courtly graces.

The young William showed a natural flair for de Tancarville's teachings. He learned to hunt in the surrounding forests, to hawk in the nearby marshes, and to handle a sword and lance under the walls of the great castle; he was instructed in singing in the chambers of de Tancarville's

"What is the function of orderly knighthood? . . . if needs must, to lay down your life."

er, had been saved from gruesome death in a siege catapult by the kindhearted King Stephen.

William Marshal had come a long way since his childhood adventure. He was now a famous warrior who commanded vast resources of wealth and soldiers, a man noted not only for his prowess in battle but also for his fierce loyalty to whichever master he happened to be serving. These were the very qualities that King Henry so desperately needed in the campaigns against his sons, and the qualities that raised a man up from a simple soldier to become a knight of the realm.

For men of William Marshal's time, knighthood was more than a career, it was a spiritual and emotional way of life. "What is the function of orderly knighthood?" asked John of Salisbury, a 12th-century philosopher, "To protect the Church, to fight against treachery, to reverence the priesthood, to fend off injustice from the poor, to make peace in your own province, to shed blood for your brethren, and if needs must, to lay down your life."

wife. All of these were essential skills for the aspiring knight.

William also learned how to survive in a royal household by shielding himself against the intrigues and shifting loyalties of the court. A successful courtier, William learned, must always keep a level head, must never show open resentment at slights from his lord, and must always be the master of his emotions. For William, whose father had consigned him to an enemy catapult without batting an eyelash, these qualities came easily. One thing William did not learn in William de Tancarville's household was how to read and write. In later life he would have to employ a kitchen clerk to keep account of his tournament winnings.

In 1167, when William had been in the household for about six years, war broke out between King Henry and King Louis of France. William, who was no more than 20, felt that the time had come to test his skills in battle, and apparently, his teacher agreed. In camp on the eve of battle, young William Marshal underwent the ritual of knighthood. His ceremony was simple and to the point—the impending conflict left no time for fanfare. Most likely he received a ritual bath, a new cloak, and a blow on the shoulder from his master—but little else.

In his first battle the following day, William demonstrated the skill and perseverance that were to mark his career. In his eagerness to be in the vanguard, the young knight very nearly overtook his master, which was considered to be bad form. "William, get back!" cried de Tancarville. "Don't be hasty!" Chastened, William paused to let his elders pass, but quickly propelled himself into the battle line, where he fought with such savagery that his lance broke under the force of his blows. It was a promising start, but William's career was almost cut short when a band of foot soldiers used an iron hook to knock him off his horse. Although William managed to fight his way free, his horse was killed.

Later, at a feast to celebrate the victory of de Tancarville's men, William may have hoped for a token of praise for his valor on the battlefield. Instead, the older knights seemed strangely derisive. "Here, Marshal!" shouted a portly earl. "I'd like a gift for love of you and reward." "Willingly," answered William. "What?" "Give me a crupper," said the old warrior, "or at least an old collar." This request for various pieces of horse tackle left William baffled. He had never owned such things, he insisted, so how could he give them away as gifts? "But Marshal," said the earl, feigning incredulity, "what are you saying? You had 40 or 60 of them—yet you refuse me so small a thing!"

William got the point: War was not fought entirely for honor; there was profit to be had in the form of ransoms for the men he defeated and the capture of their horses and arms. The gentle rebuke from his elders

A new knight receives his sword, spurs, helmet, and shield and prays that he will perform his duties well. He would then kneel before a sponsor, who would tap him lightly with a sword, bestowing upon him the honor of knighthood.

A MEDIEVAL FEMINIST

Renowned author Christine de Pisan presents a volume of her work to Isabel of Bavaria in the queen's bedchamber as ladies-in-waiting look on. Under the patronage of the queen's husband, Charles VI of France, Christine began her career by writing love poems but later turned to more serious topics, such as history, ethics, and religion.

Best remembered for her tracts in support of women, Christine wrote about heroic female figures, chastised others for contemptuous attitudes toward women, and promoted education for girls. Below, an excerpt from a poem entitled "Letter to the God of Love" compares women's behavior with men's:

> They murder no one, nor wound,
> nor harm,
> Betray men, nor pursue,
> nor seize,
> Nor houses set on fire,
> nor disinherit men,
> Nor poison, nor steal gold or silver;
> They do not cheat men of their lands,
> Nor make false contracts, nor destroy
> Kingdoms, duchies, empires . . .
> Nor wage war and kill and plunder . . .

drove the point home, especially as he had lost an expensive horse and would have to sell his new cloak to replace it. From then on, William would not be so naive.

Being a knight, he was to learn, was an expensive business. To begin with, he would need three horses—one for his baggage, another for travel, and a big-boned war-horse for battle. He must also have the long, rich cloak of a gentleman, upon which the coat of arms of his lord would be embroidered. Even more costly were the tools of war, which included a hood, a neck-and-torso protector called a hauberk, and sturdy leggings, all made of fine-meshed chain mail to protect him from spearpoints, arrows, and the sharp edge of swords. Beneath the chain mail he would wear a leather or quilted underrobe to deaden the impact of blows he received in battle. His shield, made of wood and boiled leather, and painted over with his arms, would be tied across his shoulder on a leather thong. He would also need several styles of headgear, ranging from a light iron cap over a chain mail coif to a heavy iron combat helmet with eye slits and ventilation holes, which had to be laced tightly to his shoulders for full protection in battle. A sword and a light, ashwood lance completed his battle gear.

All of which posed a problem for William. He was now a trained knight; he knew how to fight, how to dress, how to eat and drink, and how to conduct himself among the aristocracy. What he did not know was how to support himself. His time in the de Tancarville household was now at an end, and William would have to make his way in the world with no resources other than his wits.

His options were limited. As his father's youngest son, William was not entitled to a share of the family's wealth and estates. He may have considered returning home to become a "hearth son," a member of his elder brother's household, promising never to marry, and growing old with no particular direction or definition to his life. For William, who had already tasted the glories of battle, it was not a very appetizing prospect.

He chose instead to become a professional man of arms, to offer his skills and loyalty to whichever wealthy noble might bid for his services. To advertise his services, William—like many another rising young knight—entered tournaments. These mock battles were an ideal venue to earn ready cash and show off combat skills.

Tournament life was very good to William. Teamed with another knight, he captured a total of 103 knights over a span of 10 months, en-

MEDIEVAL WAR GAMES

By the end of the 11th century, a new weapon found its way onto the battlefields of Europe—the couched lance, with which a knight could strike an enemy from a distance of about five feet. But lances were unwieldy and required a great deal of practice to handle effectively. Knights soon found that mock combat provided an excellent means of training with the lance.

At first these simulated battles—called tournaments—were messy affairs in which any number of men would charge headlong at each other with lances and swords, the goal being to unhorse as many other knights as possible. Any knight who knocked another to the ground could lay claim to his opponent's horse and armor. There were few rules, and injuries and fatalities were common. But as tournaments grew in popularity, they turned from blood sport into pageant, governed by elaborate codes of conduct and attended by large crowds. By the late 1100s tournaments were often choreographed to reflect the chivalric romances of the day and were held to celebrate events like royal weddings and births.

Large-scale pageants soon gave way to smaller contests known as jousts, where individuals galloped toward each other, lances poised, across an enclosed area called a list. This change in format made it easier to determine the winner. Points

With swords and lances raised, scores of knights do mock battle in this mid-15th-century tournament *(left)*. In their enthusiasm the competitors have broken through the fence at right.

To soften the impact of a direct hit, jousters placed caps—called coronels—on their lance ends *(below)*. If there was bad blood between contestants, the coronels might be left off.

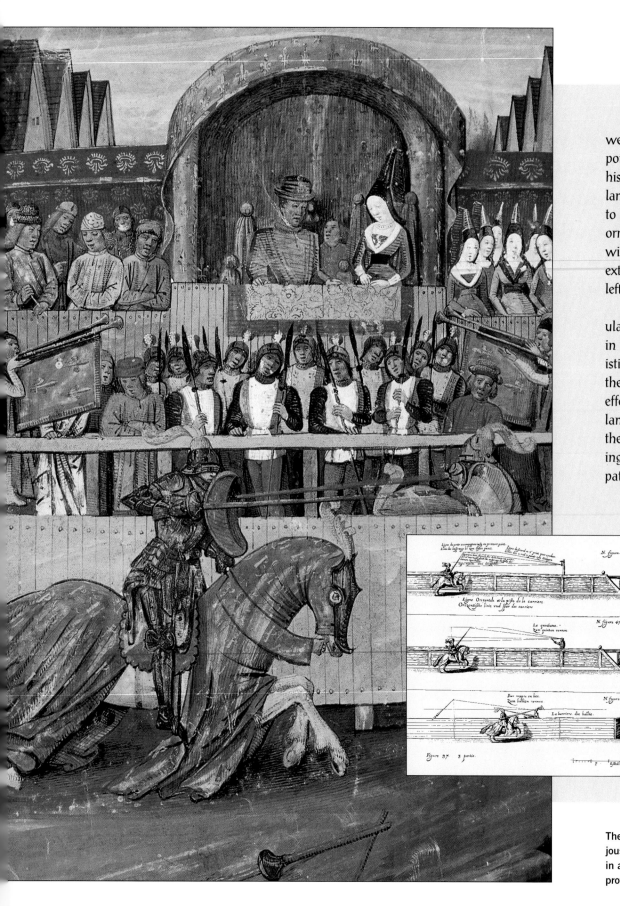

were awarded on a sliding scale; the most points went to the man who knocked a foe off his horse, with lesser scores for breaking a lance against an opponent and landing a blow to his helmet. Adding to the spectacle was the ornate armor made specifically for the joust, with sloping helmets that deflected blows and extra-thick plates that protected the knight's left side—the one exposed to the enemy.

Tournaments and jousts had faded in popularity by the start of the Thirty Years' War in 1618. There was no longer a need for realistic combat training, since new weapons in the hands of foot soldiers had diminished the effectiveness of the mounted knight and his lance. As entertainment they lost favor with their patrons in the ruling class, who increasingly felt it beneath them to view or participate in such games.

A diagram depicts three tournament contests: lancing a suspended ring *(top)*, the quintain *(middle)*, and jousting *(bottom)*. In the quintain—named for the five chances each knight was given—a knight had to strike a sandbag dummy squarely to swing it out of the way and then ride past quickly to avoid getting hit by it from behind.

The tilt, a wooden fence separating the jousters, helped keep the horses running in a straight line and also gave some protection to both animal and rider.

The tournament's victor receives his prize—a jewel adorned with ostrich feathers. But for the knight the real prize was in the horses and armor he could win from his opponents.

hancing both his reputation and his purse. Not all of the contests ended well for him. One time, William received a blow to the head that turned his helmet completely around on his shoulders. He had to find his way to the nearest blacksmith and place his head on the anvil to be pried free.

William's tournament exploits soon won him a place in the military household of a powerful uncle, Earl Patrick of Salisbury. These were the middle years of King Henry's reign, and the earl had been given the task of escorting Queen Eleanor to her private lands in Poitiers. As the party neared its destination, they were ambushed by French soldiers. The queen was rushed to safety while the knights scrambled for their arms, but before they could even mount a defense, Earl Patrick was cut down from behind.

Enraged by the cowardly attack, William rode into battle without even troubling to put on his helmet, slashing away at his uncle's murderers with furious strength. Fighting "like a wild boar amongst the dogs," William was soon knocked off his horse, surrounded, and stabbed in the leg. His captors tied him onto a horse and carted him off for ransom. This was to be the only time William Marshal was ever captured in battle.

William lacked the resources to pay his own ransom, so Queen Eleanor herself, who had been impressed by his bravery, bought his freedom and retained his services. At the tender age of 21 William Marshal had reached the pinnacle of a young knight's aspiration: service in a royal household.

Soon William transferred to the household of Eleanor's eldest son, Henry, the Young King. Here he found himself on precarious footing. The growing chasm between the Young King and his father would mean ruin for anyone who backed the wrong side. William's sympathies may have been with the father, but his loyalty had been purchased by the son. For a time William managed to walk this tightrope successfully. He became an intimate of the Young King—more of a companion than a bodyguard. Young Henry showered his friend with small gifts and favors. William eventually gained such prestige that he was able to raise his own company of knights, who wore his coat of arms— a half-green, half-yellow banner with a raging red lion. William could now be found strutting around young Henry's castle in bright robes of yellow, green, and red silk, topped with flashing jewels and brilliantly polished armor.

In 1173 the Young King offered the greatest tribute of all by asking William to knight him—an honor perhaps better reserved for his father. Here again William's diplomatic instincts served him well. Rather than dub the Young King with the traditional open-handed blow, William substituted a gentle kiss.

Soon William fell victim to his own success. Jealous courtiers spread a rumor that he had slept with the Young King's wife, Margaret. Given his ironclad sense of loyalty and personal honor, it seems unlikely that the rumor was true, but it spread uncontrollably throughout the royal household and he could do little about it. The tight-lipped stoicism that defined his knighthood prevented him from denying—or even acknowledging— such an unseemly charge.

True or not, the gossip placed William in a dangerous bind. In Flanders, when Prince Philip had discovered one of his knights in a liaison with his wife, the culprit was severely beaten and

hung head down in a sewer until he suffocated. Happily, the Young King did not react quite so vengefully. Though William had to withdraw from the royal household for a time, Henry quickly recalled him when fighting with his father and brothers heated up again.

As it happened, William rejoined the Young King just in time to see him succumb to a fatal attack of dysentery. Now William had an entirely new set of duties to perform. Under his direction, Henry's bowels, brain, and eyes were removed and the body was packed in salt and stitched into a bull's hide for its journey home. It was not a particularly regal funeral procession; the Young King's long series of campaigns against his father had left him so destitute that there was no money left over for a proper burial. William himself was seized by a band of young Henry's mercenaries demanding their arrears of pay, and only his personal pledge satisfied them that the debt would be settled.

The future could not have looked terribly bright to William as he weighed his prospects, but within three years he had found a place with King Henry himself, whose renewed difficulties with another son, Richard, left him needing battle-ready knights.

Once again, William distinguished himself on the field of battle. At Le Mans, where King Henry made his defiant last stand against Richard's forces, William staunchly held his ground against superior numbers. Here Richard made a rare and nearly fatal mistake. Thinking that his father's men were routed, Richard threw down his arms to lighten the burden on his horse and galloped ahead to claim his victory. William lay waiting in ambush, pinning the defenseless Richard at the point of his lance. The young prince, who recognized William, called out that it would be an evil deed to kill an unarmed man. William reluctantly agreed. Lowering his lance point, William killed Richard's horse and called on the devil to take care of Richard himself. It is just as well that he spared the rebellious prince; by the time William regrouped his forces, King Henry was dead.

Heraldic art developed from the practice of decorating armor in order to identify knights in the field. The lion rampant, a symbol of nobility, on the shield of William Marshal, earl of Pembroke *(shown above and at right on a drawing of Marshal's tomb effigy),* probably signifies the knight's closeness with the royal family.

Marshal's devotion to them earned him the job of guardian to young Henry III. Despite his advanced age, Marshal agreed to the task, stating, "If everyone else abandoned the king, do you know what I would do? I would carry him on my shoulders, step by step, from island to island, from country to country, and I would not fail him, even if it meant begging my bread."

William's loyalty had placed him in a precarious spot. He had served his king valiantly, but he had made an enemy of Richard, the son who was now to take his place. William assumed that his career of royal service had ended. In fact, the new king, who was already becoming renowned as Richard the Lion-Hearted, was too practical to bear a grudge. Richard admired William and immediately retained the knight for his own royal household, even granting William the honor of bearing the royal scepter at his coronation in September of 1189.

It is easy to see why a man like William appealed to the new king. Having spent his entire life in France, Richard did not much care for England—his own coronation was one of only two visits he would make in his lifetime. "I would sell London if I could find a bidder," he once declared. In William Marshal, he had found a man he could trust to keep an eye on things while he pressed his claims elsewhere. First, however, Richard had to raise William's status even further. This he did by making generous grants of land and approving an extremely fortuitous marriage to Isabel of Striguil, who was among the wealthiest heiresses in the kingdom.

As lord of Striguil, William had two imposing castles to his name and many more under his jurisdiction. But for all his wealth and influence, William was still happiest leading troops in battle, as he did in 1197 when Richard launched a fresh campaign against King Philip II of France. William was now 50 years old, but when his troops assaulted a castle at Milly-sur-Thérain, he threw himself into the thick of the action, clambering up a ladder and flattening the constable of the castle with a blow to the helmet. Tired from his exertions, William then sat down on the body of the unconscious constable while the battle raged around him.

This happy state of affairs ended in the spring of 1199 when King Richard, while surveying the defenses of a castle, took a crossbow bolt to the shoulder. He died 11 days later, leaving the throne to his brother, John. King John's reign would last 16 years, and William fared poorly under him. The king seemed to take delight in curtailing William's lands and privileges, and at one stage grew so mistrustful of the knight that he demanded two of William's sons as hostages. William bore these misfortunes with his customary dignity, eventually earning the grudging respect of the troublesome king—

a year of the boy's rule, however, with the city of Lincoln in the hands of a rebellious faction, William decided to deal with the problem in the way he knew best. He assembled a force of 406 knights and 317 crossbowmen and set off to recapture the city.

Perhaps William realized that this would be his last battle. Now in his seventies, he remained as reckless about his personal safety as he had been at his first taste of combat more than 50 years earlier. The old soldier was so eager to charge into the fray that he had to be reminded to put on his helmet. William's forces carried the day, but only

"*I am dying. . . . I cannot defend myself from death.*"

so much so that in 1216, as the king lay on his deathbed, William Marshal's name was placed at the head of the list of nobles entrusted with the care of his son Henry, the nine-year-old heir to the throne.

As royal regent, not only was William the guardian of the king, but he had also become, in many respects, the custodian of England's future. One of his first acts was to shepherd young Henry III through the ceremony of knighthood, the second time in his career he had knighted a king.

With a child on the throne, England faced a potentially volatile transition. But William Marshal's presence at the young king's side provided a comforting link to a more stable past. These years saw his power and wealth climb to new heights. He now even owned the castle at Newbury where he had been placed in the catapult basket more than six decades earlier.

As regent William headed off unrest by offering generous terms to barons willing to submit to Henry III's rule and by seeking wherever possible to undo the injustices of King John. After

after a furious battle. He emerged from the fighting with his armor dented, but his elderly body unscathed.

There would be no more lucky escapes when, two years later, a sudden illness came upon him. William realized the end was near, and planned his four months of dying as carefully as any military campaign. From his deathbed William calmly passed over the reins of government, received a final visit from the 11-year-old king, and committed his body to the religious order of the Knights Templar. Then, while an attendant rinsed his face with rose water, William said a simple farewell to his family, "I am dying. I commend you to God. I can no longer remain with you. I cannot defend myself from death." He died on May 14, 1219, with his eyes fixed resolutely on a cross.

With William Marshal's death, a proud chapter in the history of chivalry drew to a close. Not surprisingly, the most heartfelt tributes were spoken by men who had faced him in battle. "William Marshal was," said King Philip of France, "in my judgment, the most loyal man and true I have ever known."

In God's Name: The Crusades

"The frenzy of the bar-barians has devastated the churches of God in the east, and has even—shame to say—seized into slavery the holy city of Christ, Jerusalem." With these words, Pope Urban II hoped to per-suade Christians from all over Europe to join a special kind of pilgrim-age—a holy war against the Muslims who had taken over Jerusalem as they swept through the Near East spreading their new religion of Islam.

And they responded, for in the Middle Ages no layperson could rise to a greater calling than to join the Crusades. Taking up the sign of the cross, thousands of god-fearing, god-loving men and women risked death to reclaim the Holy Land from the infidels. Led by zealots armed with lit-tle more than their faith and by nobles and knights with lances and swords (like the crusader at right, seen with his mount), they became a horde "outnumbering the sand of the seashore or the stars of heaven," as one eyewitness reported, "carrying palms and bearing crosses on their shoulders." Not only did these pilgrims travel far from their homes and families, most had put all their money into the journey, believing they were earning absolution of their sins and gaining an assured place in heaven.

The crusaders lived in violent times. In the 11th century Europe was only just emerging from the Dark Ages, and warring factions preyed on one another. Brutality was common; life was hard. The sacrifices the Crusades called for must have seemed to many merely an extension of the demands of daily existence but with one attractive difference: These would bring salvation.

The First Crusade, conceived as a military action by Pope Urban II with nobles and knights serving as Christ's warriors, attracted far more common folk than anticipated. Untrained, undisciplined, and poorly led, they made up the first wave of the more than 50,000 Europeans who began the 2,000-mile overland trek. Thousands died along the way; thousands more perished trying to take two Muslim strongholds. In the next wave, knights on horseback and foot soldiers triumphantly seized several cities as they advanced toward Jerusalem. Yet they also suffered enormously: 500 died of thirst on one day alone, and their hunger grew so extreme that some ate their horses and even the flesh of the enemy. Their forbearance and bravery, however, became the example by which future generations of crusaders, including England's Richard the Lion-Hearted and the German emperor Frederick Barbarossa, took up the cross and followed the long and arduous routes portrayed in simplified form on the map at right.

TOULOUSE

Pope Urban II delivers one of many sermons exhorting the faithful to rise up and join the First Crusade to liberate the Holy City of Jerusalem. Urban promised potential crusaders that even if they did not have much money, divine mercy would provide for them.

Chronology of the Crusades

- First Crusade 1096-1099
  Jerusalem falls to the crusaders (1099)
- Second Crusade 1147-1149
  Jerusalem taken by the Muslims (1187)
- Third Crusade 1189-1192
  Richard the Lion-Hearted takes Jaffa but Jerusalem remains in Muslim hands (1191-1192)
- Fourth Crusade 1202-1204
  Crusaders sack Constantinople (1204)
- Fifth Crusade 1217-1221
- Sixth Crusade 1228-1229
  Jerusalem returns to Christian control for 15 years (1229-1244)
- Seventh Crusade 1248-1250
- Eighth Crusade 1269-1270
  Muslims seize and destroy last Christian outposts in Holy Land (1291)

A knight kneels before a monk to receive a cross to take on his journey. A crusader wore his cross until he returned home, his vow fulfilled.

COLOGNE

NUREMBERG

VERDUN

PARIS

REGENSBURG

VÉZELAY

VIENNA

BUDA

CLERMONT

LYONS

VENICE

BELGRADE

AIGUES-MORTES

GENOA

ZARA

AVIGNON

MARSEILLES

SARDINIA

ROME

CONSTANTINOPLE

NICAEA

DORYLAEUM

CAESAREA

EDESSA

BARI

OTRANTO

CAGLIARI

ICONIUM

TARSUS

ANTIOCH

MESSINA

SICILY

CYPRUS

TRIPOLI

TUNIS

BEIRUT

DAMASCUS

SIDON

TYRE

ACRE

HAIFA

M E D I T E R R A N E A N   S E A

JAFFA

JERUSALEM

DAMIETTA

MANSURA

CAIRO

Launching the Crusades

Crusading was an expensive undertaking. Many knights sought sponsors to be able to participate; others resorted to selling or mortgaging their land, thus putting their own and their families' futures in jeopardy. Robert, duke of Normandy, went so far as to pawn his entire duchy so he could join the First Crusade.

For a king the price could be staggeringly high. Louis IX of France *(opposite, top right)* spent six years away from home and during that time had to bear the financial burden of not only maintaining his household, but also paying the wages of his knights, bowmen, and sergeants, to say nothing of supplies and the construction and maintenance of fortifications in the Holy Land, as well as countless hidden costs. One tally of Louis's crusade expenditures calculated that he had spent 12 times his annual royal income.

To the crusaders' headache of funding was added the nightmare of logistics. Moving men and matériel became easier during later crusades when improvements in Mediterranean shipping made it more practical to sail to the Holy Land than to follow the overland route. Huge cargoes of food, war-horses, and weapons may have reassured the voyagers, but the journey itself may have left many an otherwise stout-hearted crusader terrified.

Knights joining a crusade paid dearly for the privilege. Their equipment and steed alone could come to twice their annual income.

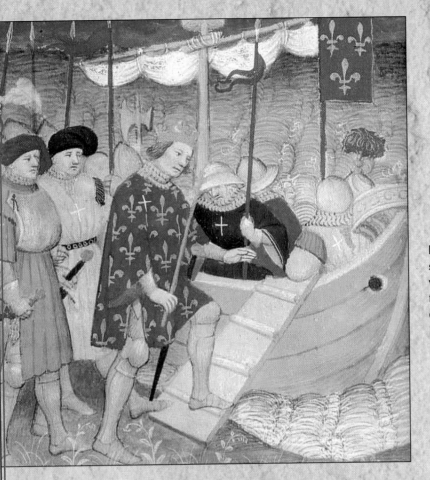

Louis IX departs on crusade. He converted a tiny village into a major port for the shipping of his equipment and supplies.

Pope Innocent III placed collection chests, such as the one below, in every church to raise funds for the crusaders.

Defensive Gear

To protect themselves from Muslim arrows, mounted knights wore iron helmets and shirts and leggings of chain mail. But their armor weighed them down and gave the more lightly clad enemy on their swift horses the advantage in cavalry battles.

"If those are blessed who die in the Lord, how much more blessed are those who die for the Lord."

Jerusalem, Pawn in a Holy War

When the earliest crusaders beheld Jerusalem for the first time on June 7, 1099, it lay sparkling in the sunshine like a vision of heaven. Deeply moved, they fell to their knees and offered thanks to God for bringing them there. But they must have known in their hearts that taking the walled city, one of the most heavily fortified of its day, would be far from easy. Having trusted in God to provide for their needs, the 13,000 besiegers soon themselves became besieged. Unable to mount the walls because they had no scaling ladders, they found themselves with very little food, water, and other provisions. Shrewdly, the city's defenders had taken the precaution of filling up or poisoning the local wells. But then, almost miraculously, a fleet of English and Genoese ships suddenly appeared off the coast, bringing both carpenters and wood with which to build ladders and mobile

towers so they could gain the ramparts.

On July 10, after these structures had been put together, the crusaders attacked, advancing slowly through a volley of flaming arrows, all the while inching their cumbersome towers toward the forbidding

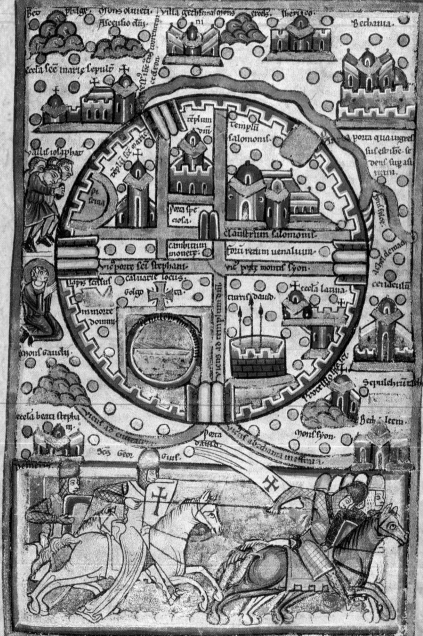

walls. Five days later one of the platforms stood in place, and the men began pouring into Jerusalem.

Inside the Holy City, the crusaders took their swords and slashed at the civilians fleeing before them, "killing them and dismembering them," and showing no mercy even to women and children. The leaders of the action wrote to the Pope, "If you want to know what was done to the enemies we found in the city, know this: that in the portico of Solomon and in His Temple, our men rode in the blood of the Saracens up to the knees of their horses." After Jerusalem fell on the 15th, the dead were so numerous that their bodies formed funeral pyres "as big as houses." Where once an estimated 20,000 Muslims and Jews had lived, none now remained.

Knowing that a Mus-

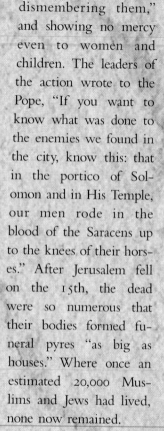

A 13th-century map of Jerusalem portrays some of the city's religious monuments, among them Christ's tomb (bottom left); the Islamic mosque (top right); and below that, the Tower of David, Jerusalem's citadel.

The Brutal Aftermath

Sanctioned, they believed, by God, the First Crusade knights killed all they met in Jerusalem. A 12th-century historian reported that "one could not, nonetheless, look on that multitude of corpses without horror, scattered arms and legs heaped on the floor on all sides."

Attacking Jerusalem, the crusaders met fierce resistance from the Muslims. But with the aid of ladders and wooden towers, they scaled the walls and took the city.

lim army was on its way to Jerusalem, a contingent of crusaders, still flushed with victory, marched out of the city to meet the advancing troops at Ashqelon on July 29. Though the Christian forces numbered only 5,000 cavalry and 15,000 infantry against the far more numerous enemy, the crusaders held the day, killing thousands and driving the survivors into retreat.

Of the triumphant crusade commanders, it fell to Godfrey of Bouillon to remain and rule Jerusalem and its outlying districts. Godfrey resisted being called king, finding the title presumptuous in the city of Christ, preferring instead to be referred to as Defender of the Holy Sepulcher. The task awaiting the new leader was formidable. With Jerusalem now under Christian control, most of the crusaders returned to their homes in Europe, which left Godfrey with just 300 knights and 2,000 infantrymen to defend the territory. Before he could prove himself equal to the task, however, he died, and the job fell to his brother, Baldwin, who did not hesitate to call himself king.

Over the next two centuries the Christians holding the crusader states that sprang up along a 600-mile corridor between the

Drums and horns signaled the Muslims' final assault on Acre. They later hung Christian heads from their horses' necks to present to the sultan.

86

mountains and the Mediterranean faced the constant threat of attack. The Muslims were unable to forget the infamy of the taking of Jerusalem, which they regarded, after Mecca and Medina, as "the third most holy place of God," the spot from which their prophet Muhammad ascended into heaven. In 1187 Jerusalem fell to the brilliant Muslim commander Saladin. The loss of the city came as such a shock to Pope Urban III that he dropped dead upon hearing the news.

For the crusaders this was the beginning of the end. Though Jerusalem would be regained in 1229, the victory proved short lived. Jerusalem yet again came under Muslim domination in 1244. And 47 years later, in 1291, an enormous army that had set out from Egypt besieged the Christian port city of Acre. Protected by a double ring of walls, the 800 knights and 14,000 foot soldiers inside put up a good fight, but were no match in the end for the hundreds of heavy stones and firebombs the attackers hurled into the city from dozens of catapults. After seven weeks of siege, Acre capitulated and the Muslims entered it, avenging themselves on the populace. "They were beheaded around Acre to the last man," an Arab chronicler wrote of the vanquished, and then "the city of Acre was demolished and razed to the ground."

Within a matter of months, the last remaining Christian strongholds fell to the Muslims. Crusading as a militant act of pilgrimage to the Holy Land was over.

Coming Home

When they returned, some crusaders found their wives waiting for them *(below)*, their homes and livelihoods intact. Greedy relatives and neighbors often preyed on the men's families, usurping their property. Few crusaders came back rich; some had little more to show for their suffering than a small cross like the one above.

For the man who failed at God's work, no worse fate could await him than the contempt of his countrymen. And when an entire crusade failed, the whole community shared the blame, for surely it was their own sinfulness that had caused God to withhold his blessing from the venture.

CHAPTER THREE

To the Manor Born

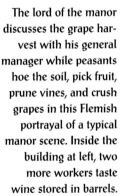

The lord of the manor discusses the grape harvest with his general manager while peasants hoe the soil, pick fruit, prune vines, and crush grapes in this Flemish portrayal of a typical manor scene. Inside the building at left, two more workers taste wine stored in barrels.

brahil was as earthy as the soil that he worked. It blackened his fingernails and was ground into the creases of his thin flesh and the rough wool of his leggings, tunic, and hood. At night he slept on a hard dirt floor, and every morning when he went outside, the first thing that he saw was the life-giving earth, spread out in rolling fields and walled in by forest. In the gray winter dawns those fields lay in black ridges crusted with frost. If it was a good year, the first green shoots of autumn wheat showed early in February, as thinly scattered as new grass. By the time the cuckoo's song could be heard in the woods, the summer barley and oats had sprouted. And in late May the fields were a solid, pale blue green. Patches of other crops—peas and beans, sheets of blue flax—lay among the wheat and barley. But it was the grain, the staff of life, that mattered most. And although his masters tried to discourage the practice, it was for the grain that he prayed to the spirits of the earth.

Abrahil's masters had good reason for trying to end such paganism—they were the monks of the Abbey of Saint-Germain des Prés near Paris. But the monks' concerns were not spiritual alone. For along with the emperor Charlemagne and other lords and prelates, they were among the great landowners of ninth-century Europe. One of their

properties was at Neuillay, 150 miles southwest of Paris, and it was here that Abrahil lived.

According to a detailed estate survey made by Irminon, the abbot of Saint-Germain, sometime between 806 and 829, Neuillay was a 130-acre clearing of plowland and meadows, surrounded by a forest of oak, beech, maple, and birch. To make sure that the land yielded up its wealth, landlords like the monks of Saint-Germain were developing a new form of management. It was known as the manorial system.

The manor was an entire estate, its land divided into two parts: the demesne, which was the landlord's own land, and a much larger area that was leased as farms to peasants. To help pay for their plots, the peasants contributed produce to the lord and worked part time on his demesne; with whatever time was left over they worked their own land.

The manorial system dominated rural life throughout the Middle Ages. Although deeply conservative, it was continually—if slowly—changing. Out of it would grow village communities of people who were largely self-governing and more and more in control of their own lives. Some among them would become rich landowners themselves, an entirely new class of people arising from the old system.

Abrahil knew little of the vast structure that was shaping the society in which he lived. He probably had heard of the emperor far away in his palace at Aachen, near the great Rhine River. And once a year he made the long journey to Paris, delivering firewood to the Abbey of Saint-Germain. But tied to the earth as he was, Abrahil's world was centered on the manorial estate, where he eked out his living as best he could.

Spring was a particularly busy season for Abrahil, when he was obliged to work much of the time on the abbey's demesne

A peasant's daily work was dictated by the demands of the seasons of the year, as depicted in the agricultural calendar at left. To perform their tasks, workers could rely on various farming implements, such as scythes and shovels. But no tool was more important to farming than the heavy-wheeled plow. The plow shown at right is a late-medieval model, as evidenced by the padded horse collar, an improvement that allowed the speedier horse to replace the ox as a draft animal.

in addition to his own fields. That meant reporting to the steward, the man who ran the estate for the abbot. Knowing that he must not be late, Abrahil would rise early, no doubt stiff after a night on a straw pallet on the tamped-down mud.

In the faint light that came in through small, unglazed windows, Abrahil looked around him at the one-room hut in which he and his family had spent the night. It was a flimsy affair, a post-and-beam structure with walls of wickerwork filled in with mud. A table, a chest, and a bench or two were the only furniture. The place must have smelled, for it was also home to Abrahil's chickens, sheep, and pigs, and a pungent manure pile sat uncomfortably close to the door.

In the center of the room Abrahil could see the open hearth, where his wife had cooked the previous evening's meal, often soup or porridge. All the heat that the fire had provided was gone now, of course, vanished like the smoke that had escaped through a hole in the thatched roof.

Stretching his muscles, Abrahil got ready to leave. Still asleep, perhaps, were his three children, but not his wife, who faced a workday at least as arduous as his. Her name was Berthildis, and in accordance with Frankish custom, the children's names were variants of hers and Abrahil's: Abram and Avremarus for the boys, and Bertrada for the girl.

According to Abbot Irminon's survey, Abrahil was a slave. We do not know the reason for his lowly status; he may have been a slave simply because his father had been one. Berthildis was listed as a half-free woman and could have been a former slave whose obligations were lightened. Also on the estate at Neuillay were freemen, but they, too, were bound to the manor, having surrendered their own land in exchange for protection by the lord. Indeed, these classifications were ceasing to mean much at manors like Neuillay, where all the categories were merging into one class of tenant, the serf.

In front of a dwelling that was home to valuable livestock as well as humans, a peasant couple perform a regular household chore, chopping and gathering firewood.

Bidding goodbye to his wife, Abrahil would head off toward the steward's big house. This was a three- or four-room stone house located in the center of Neuillay. Surrounding it were a number of other farm buildings—barns, stables, a bakehouse, a kitchen—as well as the wooden huts in which the household slaves lived and worked.

The walk from Abrahil's home to the steward's house was not a long one. Along the way, others would join him, carrying spades, pitchforks, rakes, and scythes. If it was Abrahil's job to plow that day, he may have used one of the newer plows of the period; these had colters to slice the sod, share beams and iron plowshares to dig it, wooden moldboards for turning the furrow over, and stilts for adjusting course and depth. But most people still worked with a light scratch plow that literally only scratched the surface and required cross plowing and then spading to turn the soil.

Peasants throughout the medieval world realized their dependence on the soil, and even had a deep reverence for it, but they understood very little about how to maintain its fertility. Manure was scarce, used mostly for kitchen gardens, and the concept of replenishing the soil by planting crops such as alfalfa and clover was unknown. People did know about crop rotation, however: Generations of experience had taught them that if the earth did not lie fallow it would be exhausted after a couple of years of cultivation. In fact, Abrahil probably already worked with the three-field rotation that would become the pattern all across Europe: One field sowed in autumn for winter wheat, one in the early months of the year for summer oats and barley, and one left fallow to restore itself.

At the demesne Abrahil, more than likely a robust figure of about five foot five, would have plowed all day, steadily walking behind a team of oxen and cutting the land into the characteristic pattern of ridge and furrow. Spring days like this one were pleasant, but he was used to working in all weather, as his leathery, weather-beaten face attested. Who knows what thoughts would have occupied him during his long hours in the fields? No doubt often on his mind was the steward, or his assistants, who could inflict penalties on him—and even have him flogged—if he thought

Metal was both scarce and valuable, so the iron cauldron at left probably belonged to a wealthy landowner. The pots and tableware of the poor generally were made of earthenware or wood, like the pitcher and spoon below.

Abrahil was slacking. Clearly it was important to maintain a good relationship with such a powerful manor figure; a small gift of eggs would often help matters, although the abbot of Saint-Germain tolerated such practices less than most other landlords.

He may have thought about the abbot and his monks, with their clean shirts, drawers, hooded capes, stockings, warm cloaks, and sheepskin mittens. While the monks were issued a new wardrobe every year, Abrahil had no changes of clothes, wearing the same dirt-caked tunic and leggings until they fell apart.

Like many a laboring man, food was never far from his mind. Indeed, only to eat his meal would he cease his labors, perhaps gathering together with the other workers under the shade of a tree. He knew that his masters dined better than he did, on white bread; cheeses; game from the forests; fish from manorial ponds; as well as the mutton, pork, chicken, duck, and goose provided by the serfs. For drink, they had wine from the vineyards. Abrahil consoled himself with his own food: coarse rye or mixed-grain bread, grain stews, and vegetables from his garden plot, all washed down with ale or water. Occasionally he had pork.

It was not a complete diet, and even in good years it provided barely enough iron for a man; women, whose iron requirements are twice that of men, often suffered from pernicious anemia and the potentially fatal diseases it left them vulnerable to. Many years were not good, however. Abrahil probably recalled the famine of 791, for example, when serfs were reduced to eating whatever they could find—earth mixed with flour, roots, their horses, and even, it is said, each other.

Memories of such difficult times may have helped Abrahil bear his present burdens, substantial as they were. He was responsible for a yearlong calendar of manor chores that included harvesting, carting manure, and transporting firewood to nearby towns. Payments were also due to the master for a whole host of rights, such as cutting wood and foraging pigs in the master's forest, grazing cattle on the stubble of his fields, and grinding grain in his mills. In addition he must pay a tithe to the church and an army tax—the price of avoiding military service—of "2 muttons, 8 chickens, 30 eggs, 100 planks and shingles, 12 staves, 6 hoops, and 12 torches."

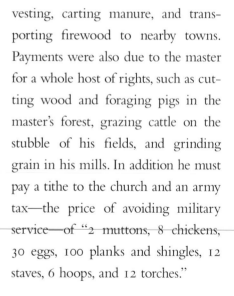

While others wait their turn, a peasant, his knees bent in humility, pays his dues—money, goods, or livestock—to the lord of the manor.

In return, the abbey granted Abrahil a tract of nearly 50 acres of arable land with a small meadow, which he shared with two other families. It was here that he would toil longest and hardest.

To help get through a day in the fields, Abrahil and his fellow laborers sang heartily. As they tilled the soil, they would recite ancient charms and incantations, praying to Mother Earth for an abundant harvest, for the health of a sick child, or for the easing of their own painful muscles and joints. Indeed, through these very fields they may have danced, dressed as beasts, seeking a blessing on the land. And in the deep, haunted forests surrounding the clearings, they would gather in sacred groves to make animal sacrifices to the gods of old.

But by now, Abrahil's mind was on food again. The rumbling in his belly told him that his day of toil was almost over, and soon the weary worker would be making his way back home for a well-earned dinner.

Since he left, early that morning, Berthildis had been equally hard at work. Hitching up her loose gown, she may have spent the day cooking, spinning, or weaving the woolens that would be needed for the coming winter. Or, donning her hood and tossing a cloak around her shoulders, perhaps she had been tending the chickens or shearing sheep or toiling in the vegetable garden. And it was she, of course, who took care of the children.

But as the sun slipped below the wooded horizon, all work came to an end and the family settled down for another night on the hard earth. In exceptional circumstances Abrahil may have lighted one of his handmade candles to prolong the light, but this was rare. Candles were prohibitively expensive and would be needed more during the long winter evenings. Besides, Abrahil and Berthildis would have to rise early the next morning, too, and sleep would not be long in coming.

A look at an English manorial village shows what the system had become by the end of the 13th century. The village we will consider is Elton, located about 70 miles north of London in some of the most fertile land in the country.

What we know about life at Elton comes from three main sources: the court records, the accounts of the manor, and a roy-

Pushed to extremes by hard work and heavy taxes, ax-wielding peasants exact revenge on a representative of the ruling classes, a solitary knight.

HEALTH AND HEALING IN THE MIDDLE AGES

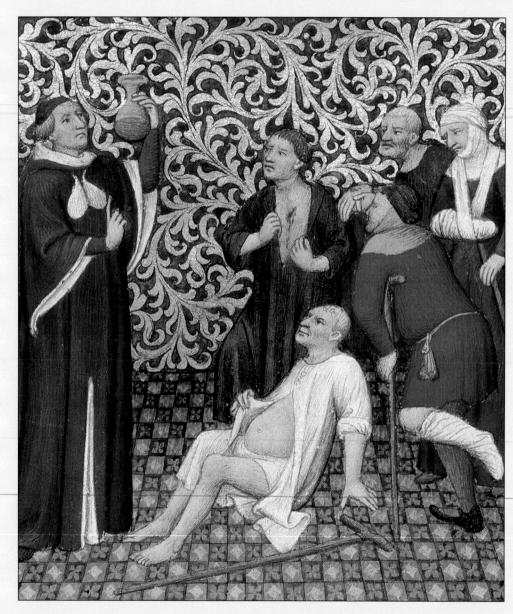

A formally trained physician, identifiable by his splendid robes, uses the widespread diagnostic technique of examining a patient's urine.

The people of the Middle Ages were afflicted with many of the same sicknesses, from cancer to nosebleeds, that exist today. But they also had to contend with a variety of skin lesions and other ailments that are no longer the scourges they once were. Diseases such as smallpox, leprosy, St. Anthony's fire, and St. Vitus's dance were products of the unsanitary living conditions, overcrowding, and malnutrition that characterized the lives of the majority of Europe's population.

At that time disease was thought to result from an imbalance in the four fluids, or humors, of the body—choler, phlegm, black bile, and blood. The physician's task was to restore the balance of these humors. Means at his disposal included cauterization, surgery, diet, and medicine. A common medical practice was bloodletting, in which a specific vein was opened to treat a particular disease. The blood was then checked for distinctive properties, such as smell or greasiness.

Medical science during the Middle Ages became increasingly sophisticated and even extended to the study of cadavers. Profusely illustrated manuals guided apprentice doctors through every step of patient diagnosis. There were charts to aid in inspecting urine for color, smell, and sedimentation; calendars and tables for use in astrological medicine; manuals on techniques of bloodletting; pharmaceutical reference books depicting herbs and their applications; and collections of recipes for balms and potions.

Members of the medical community ranged from university-trained doctors—strongly influenced by centuries of Greek and Islamic insight—to traditional healers, who learned their craft through apprenticeship to other folk practitioners. The care provided by a formally trained doctor was priced beyond the reach of most people, although in the early 13th century some Italian cities retained physicians to treat the poor for free. And during the 14th and 15th centuries, religious communities offered the poor and aged refuge in hospitals, providing food, shelter, and prayer, along with limited medical care. On the whole, however, during the Middle Ages such care for agrarian peasants and poor city dwellers alike was limited to the ministrations of village healers, herbalists, and barber-surgeons, as well as to self-medication and visits to mineral baths.

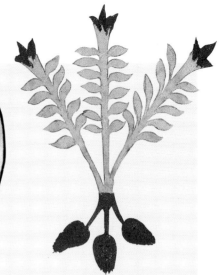

A woman holds a bowl to catch blood spurting from a blood-letting incision on her arm.

A 14th-century illustration identifies the herb foltas, used to treat epilepsy. Physicians prescribed local plants for poorer patients, but more exotic herbs for the affluent.

A physician conducts a hands-on examination, which could reveal abscesses, swellings, or tumors.

This guidebook of diagnosis and treatment was worn at a physician's waist. It also had astrological charts to predict the outcome of an illness.

al survey carried out in 1279. From these a picture of a prosperous village emerges, its thatched, wattle-and-daub houses and cottages clustered between the manor house and the Nene River, all surrounded by a patchwork of fields.

Like Neuillay 400 years earlier, Elton was one of the manors that provided income for an abbey, in this case nearby Ramsey Abbey. And as at Neuillay, the abbot had a demesne, with about 400 acres of arable land, 16 acres of meadow, three of pasture, two water mills on the Nene, and a mill for fulling, or cleaning, wool. The rest of the arable land—approximately 1,400 acres—was divided among village tenants, many of whom owed the landlord regular "week work" (usually about three days a week) and seasonal "boon work" (extra labor for peak periods of the year).

In other ways, though, Elton was very different from Neuillay. For one thing, all its villagers were not equal. Somehow, in the development of manor custom, English villagers had acquired rights to inheritance and to buy and sell land. And while most villagers had only cottages with small gardens, some had managed to acquire large amounts of land. John of Elton, for example, farmed 144 acres and even had tenants of his own.

But despite their holdings, all 500 residents of Elton were still subject to the lord of the manor, the abbot of Ramsey, and his steward. But by now the villagers had an official to represent them, one chosen by them and from among their own number: the reeve.

The reeve was a kind of village headman, although his loyalties were split—a villager himself, but one responsible to the lord of the manor. Among his duties were supervising labor and work teams, overseeing livestock, collecting manorial rents, selling produce, and rendering yearly accounts.

To help him he had various assistants, such as a woodward, to guard the manor woods, and a hayward, who was in charge of the hedges and fences. The symbol for the latter's office was a horn, which—like the hayward Little Boy Blue—he blew as a warning when farm animals got into the crops.

In return, the reeve enjoyed considerable compensation. For example, he was freed from the week work owed on his land, could use the lord's horses or oxen for his own plowing, and was permitted to graze his animals in demesne pasture.

In such circumstances there was plenty of opportunity for illicit self-enrichment; in fact, the great English poet Geoffrey Chaucer made corrupt reeves immortal in his *Canterbury Tales*. And so perhaps it is not surprising to learn from the court rolls that the reeve of Elton was accused of irregularities of conduct.

The official in question was Michael Reeve, whose surname, like many that began to appear for the first time during this century, came from the office that he held. One Sunday afternoon at the end of October 1278, Reeve later charged, three fellow villagers confronted him in Elton's churchyard, "with most base words in front of the whole parish." They may well have been drinking, for Elton men were known for their alcohol consumption, downing as much as two gallons of ale each in a single day. In any case, in the scene that rapidly developed outside the church, the trio accused Reeve of abusing his office. In particular, they claimed that he had been taking bribes, using tenants to harvest and plow his own land, and excusing some tenants from carting services if they leased their lands to him cheaply. Reeve was furious at their allegations. He had a recourse, though: He took them all to court for libel.

The hallmoot, or manorial court, was a unique legal body that met every three weeks to handle all litigation other than cases involving canon law—taken care of in church courts—or crimes like murder and treason, which went to the royal courts. The abbot's steward presided and gave the hallmoot authority, but it was the villagers who ran it.

The case against Michael Reeve would have been investigated by jurors—village officials who collected evidence, looked into law and custom, made judgments, and decided penalties. In this trial they found in Reeve's favor, declaring that he was "in no ar-

THE LEGEND OF ROBIN HOOD

Over the years, Robin Hood has been depicted in many guises: As a yeoman, or officer in a noble household *(left)*; as a nobleman himself, one unlawfully denied his inheritance; as an Anglo-Saxon patriot defending his homeland against the conquering Normans; and finally as the character that we know today, the romantic bandit who fought for the common people against their greedy landlords.

Historical evidence for a fugitive from justice named Robin Hood dates back to 1296, and a number of medieval ballads and plays feature an outlaw by that name. But the noble figure who robbed from the rich and gave to the poor remains elusive—a myth-clad scoundrel who has robbed history of his true identity.

ticle guilty." His accusers were then told to pay him damages of ten shillings. But having cleared his name, Reeve was quick to make his peace with the three defendants, forgiving them everything but two shillings. He had to live with these people, after all.

The hallmoot was known to take a hard line against physical violence. Assaulting someone in his own house, known as hamesucken *(or hamsoken),* was considered especially serious: "Matilda Saladin justly raised the hue-and-cry upon five men of Sir Gilbert de Lyndsey who were committing hamsoken upon Philip Saladin and beat and badly treated him," runs one dramatic entry in the court rolls. When someone raised the hue and cry, all within earshot were required to drop whatever they were doing and help. Failure to do so brought fines for everyone nearby. So did falsely raising the hue and cry, or crying wolf.

Fines were also imposed for the improper sale and brewing of ale. Women all up and down the village street brewed it, then displayed a sign outside their doors to indicate they were open for business. But they could be prosecuted if they charged too much for the ale or if their brews were too weak. Judging from the long lists of fines, there seem to have been plenty of culprits.

Most court cases, however, had to do with work. A multitude of issues required rulings: How much was owed in fines by tenants who refused their week or boon work, what was owed when someone's plow encroached on someone else's land, what work was or was not owed the lord. Throughout the proceedings there was never any doubt that the lord was in authority. But it was equally understood that if the lord infringed on the villagers' customary rights—by demanding noncustomary work, for instance—then the whole village would be up in arms, and in court.

For the most part, though, the manorial system worked because all the community labored together throughout the year. Increasing trade with nearby market towns supplied the manor

THE MAID OF ORLÉANS

Some 90 years into the Hundred Years' War, a young peasant girl named Joan was called upon to perform a great service for her beleaguered country. The commission, which she claimed came from God himself, was to deliver France from the hands of the English.

Short and sturdy, with black hair and a ruddy complexion, the girl seemed an unlikely national savior. Like the other children in her poor village in northeastern France, she had a daily routine that included household and farm chores and taking part in the occasional festivals that brightened an otherwise harsh existence. But in time her countrymen would call this seemingly unremarkable child the Maid of Orléans, and history would know her as Joan of Arc.

Joan was just 13 years old when, she later said, "God sent a voice to guide me." Joan heard the voices frequently over the next few years, and eventually she determined to heed their call to action. In January of 1429 she

Clad in armor and holding her sword, Joan of Arc prepares to fight for the man she thought the rightful king of France, Charles VII (inset). Behind her is the standard she carried into battle.

Joan's helmet—which was similar to the one at right—would become a votive offering in an Orléans church.

made her way to the Loire Valley, where Charles VII of France—successor to a throne denied him by the English–held court. There, in a man's black tunic and boots and with her hair cropped short, she addressed Charles: "The King of Heaven," she declared, "sends me to you with the message that you shall be anointed and crowned in the city of Reims." She continued, "Will you believe that I am sent by God?"

Whether Charles believed or not, Joan managed to win his backing for her cause. Hundreds of others had no doubts and flocked to her banner, a white satin standard with images of Christ, the world, two angels, and the lilies of France. Heartened, Joan set out to raise the English siege of Orléans, 70 miles southwest of Paris.

Led by Joan, the French army successfully made its way through hostile territory and in May 1429 drove the English from Orléans. After a series of victories against the enemy in the Loire, Joan and her followers entered Reims. There, less than six months after she had left her village, Joan witnessed the highlight of her life, the coronation of Charles VII.

Once the ceremony was over, however, Joan was anxious to march on Paris.

Banner aloft, Joan leads her followers to a meeting with Charles, hoping to persuade him to continue the war against England.

But she would have to wage this campaign without the support of the king, who was reluctant to fight on. Soon Joan's military fortunes began to falter: Her attack on Paris failed, and during a battle north of the city the following spring, she fell into the hands of the English. Joan then discovered that she had more enemies than those she faced on the field of battle: Concluding that her voices were more likely from the devil than from God, the vicar-general of the Inquisition demanded that she be tried for witchcraft and heresy. In the end both camps passed judgment on her: On May 29, 1431, the French bishops excommunicated her, and on May 30 the English army burned her at the stake.

Twenty-five years after the execution, Pope Calixtus III annulled Joan's guilty verdict. Her rehabilitation had begun. The process would not be complete until 1920, when another pope, Benedict XV, canonized her a saint, reclaiming for God the young peasant woman that the church had condemned 500 years before.

Eyes on a crucifix, Joan awaits death at the stake. Fearing damnation for burning a saint, her executioner *(left)* would later flee to a monastery.

Though unable to read or write, Joan—or in French, Jehanne—could sign her name, as evidenced by her signature on this 1429 letter.

with all kinds of goods, such as salt for curing meat, iron for the manor's blacksmith, and thatch for roofs (the latter was a good insulator but needed frequent replacement). On the other hand, there was a growing market for the manor's wool, and English wool was particularly prized for its fineness. But 13th-century landlords had not yet realized that their land might be more profitable supporting sheep than growing grain.

Food crops still retained a primary, even a mystic importance. To the church fathers, in fact, country life seemed ingrained with paganism. They knew that organized religion had laid only a thin veneer of Christianity over the land and that besides Christian holy days,

(often women) could be seen striding through the fields that had been left fallow the previous season. Carried in baskets or in the folds of their garments were seeds for winter wheat and rye, which they broadcast by hand over the rejuvenated earth.

After sowing came the feast of All Saints and All Souls, on November 1 and 2. These were the Christian versions of the Celtic feast Samhain, the day that divided the warm and the cold season, the light and the dark. And as a division—a space between two different periods, neither one nor the other—the Celts saw it as a doorway between the spirit and the actual world. All sorts of creatures were free to roam on Samhain: The Welsh said a ghost sat on every stile that night.

"Matilda Saladin justly raised the hue-and-cry upon five men . . . who were committing hamsoken upon Philip Saladin."

villagers would celebrate other festivals, many as old as farming itself. Associated with the solstices and the equinoxes, they tended to fall just after the great periods of work.

Unable to prevent such ancient festivals, the church eventually absorbed them. Just as it had transformed many of the old gods into saints, so the church incorporated these holidays into the Christian calendar, often without changing them much. And as the manorial system evolved during the Middle Ages, these festivals came to mark official turning points in the farming year.

Crop cultivation began at the end of September, when the previous year's harvest was done; the cattle were turned loose to graze on the stubble; and Michael Reeve was busy rendering his accounts, using tally sticks to keep track. It was then that tenants

As the year drew to its end, the last of the grain had been threshed and winnowed in the great barns, and darkness had closed in around the manor. This was the dead season. Although the Germanic yule celebrated the returning sun after the winter solstice, field work had by now almost stopped. From Christmas Eve to Twelfth Night, in fact, there were no obligations for the villagers, other than the customary donation of hens for the lord's table. But it was then that the lord would give feasts for his tenants, sometimes providing a single villager with "two white loaves, as much beer as they will drink in the day, a mess of beef and of bacon with mustard."

January was the month when repair work was carried out on fences, barns, and hedges, just as farmers still do today. Actual field work began again after Candlemas, on February 2, a holy day associated with the Purification of the Virgin. Named after the women's custom of carrying candles to church for purification after childbirth, Candlemas had replaced a pagan feast called Imbolc, which may have marked the season when ewes came into milk. Now the field that had been sown with winter wheat and rye the year before was plowed and sown with the summer crops; oats and barley were planted on the ridges of the plowed furrow, peas and beans between.

There was also May Day—the old fertility festival of Beltane—when blossoming white hawthorn was brought indoors to celebrate the spring, and Whitsunday (Pentecost), the seventh Sunday after Easter, the start of a whole week's holiday.

By this time of year the weather was warming. As the trees came into leaf and the meadows bloomed, the grain ripened and the pace of work quickened. For the farming year was now moving toward its climax, signaled by the bonfires and the burning wheels that villagers rolled down hills to mark Midsummer Night, the solstice, which the church called St. John's Eve. After that, haymaking began, first on the lord's demesne and then on the villagers' own sections of meadow. The cutting, stacking, and drying of the hay all had to be finished by August 1, the start of harvest, which in times past had been marked by the pagan celebration Lugnasadh. Now the day was known as Lammas, an Anglo-Saxon phrase meaning "loaf mass," for the loaves baked from the first new grain.

This was the busiest time of the year for everyone in the village, when the grain had to be gathered in swiftly, as soon as the ears bent heavily on

Village taverns sprang up, replacing private alehouses. Minstrels and troubadours entertained patrons with songs like this one from the *Carmina Burana:*

Once for the buyer of the wine
free men drink out of it;
twice they drink for those in gaol,
after that, three times for the living,
four times for all Christians,
five times for those who died in the Faith,
six times for the weak sisters,
seven times for the forces on forest duty.

Eight times for errant brothers,
nine times for monks dispersed,
ten times for sailors,
eleven times for quarrellers,
twelve times for penitents,
thirteen times for those going on a journey,
the same for the Pope as for the king,
everyone drinks without licence.

the stalks. During this peak period the workdays owed the abbot increased, and laborers from outside the manor were even brought in to help with the harvest.

The reeve had to oversee it all, keeping track of the people called on to work off their boon, and recording the agreements about the gleaning of the shorn fields by the poor and the dates when cattle would be let back in to graze.

These were urgent, stressful days. Yet there was a real harmony in the constant rhythm of villagers toiling on the land. Reapers advanced across the golden fields in long lines, bending with short sickles to cut wheat halfway up the stalk or swinging scythes to mow oats and barley close to the ground. They laid the golden stalks in piles as they went. Behind them came binders, one for every four reapers, each group moving at a pace of two acres a day, gathering the grain into shocks and setting them up to dry.

Later the beans and peas would be harvested. But it was those long summer days, when they moved in concert among the grain, that symbolized harvest to most people. For it was on the grain—the fruits of the earth on which they labored through the year—that life depended. And it was the harvest that made the village a community: When the work on the demesne was done, they could turn together to their own fields.

The abbot's return for all the villagers' boon work were the feasts given in celebration of each day of the harvest. Again it was up to the reeve to keep account of everything. In 1298, for instance, the harvest at Elton lasted two and a half days. On the first day, 329 people worked. They were fed bread and porridge made from 32 bushels of wheat and roughly the same amount of oats and barley; meat from 18 doves, a calf, a cow, and a bull; seven cheeses; and oceans of beer. On the second day, when fewer workers were needed, 250 people got bread, herrings, salt cod, cheese, and beer. The leftovers went to the 60 who brought the harvest to its great conclusion on the final day.

Such yearly fortune was the result of a system of land management perhaps best suited to the times, which were uncertain, and the technology, which was undeveloped. And from this system, in the century that followed, would arise families that, even in the worst of times, amassed amazing wealth and produced memorable personalities. These newly successful families were part of the landed gentry. Among them, few were more remarkable than the Pastons of Norfolk county, and among the Pastons, few could match Margaret, one of the most formidable women of her—or any—age.

The rise of the Pastons into the gentry was a comparatively recent development. The family had taken its name from a small village in the east of England near the windswept coastal marshes of the North Sea. There, sometime in the 14th century, a plowman named Clement Paston began to amass land.

That the Pastons not only survived in this period, but thrived, is proof of their vitality, their shrewdness, and their sheer determination. For the family lived in terrible times. This was a century wracked by warfare between France and England—the Hundred Years' War—and half-ruined by the horrors of the bubonic plague from which, according to a chronicler of the day, "one-third of Europe's population perished." But it was followed by an even worse one.

Twenty-two years into the next century, England's capable King Henry V died, leaving as his successor an infant son who, as it turned out, suffered from periodic insanity. Ironically, the very success of Henry's reign—the hero of the Battle of Agincourt had built a vast empire by conquest—had demonstrated to the lords of the land that war was the way to fortune. And it was Henry's son who would suffer. During the new monarch's reign, the kingdom was really controlled by various land magnates, who found to their delight that they could squabble, help themselves to the royal revenue, and use the system of justice for their own ends. The result was the Wars of the Roses, which occupied most of the rest of the violence-ridden century.

Even so, the rise of the money economy and the flourishing of education in the 15th century provided opportunities for the ambitious and hardworking. Conditions were particularly good for lawyers. Perhaps because he was used to village litigiousness, Clement Paston wisely had his son William educated as a jurist, and the young man did not disappoint him. William became a wealthy and distinguished judge in the royal courts. And like his father, he, too, began to acquire land. One way he did this was by marrying, which he did fairly late in life, at 42. His bride, Agnes Berry, was about half his age, the heiress of a Hertfordshire knight.

This medieval game, a forerunner of baseball, was played with a semispherical ball that was probably made of cloth or leather and was filled with bran.

HOLIDAY REVELRY

Seasonal fairs, markets, and country festivals offered a much-needed respite from the daily grind of farm labor. Bands of dancers, jugglers, acrobats, puppeteers, and musicians traveled from village to village to perform at the numerous outdoor celebrations held during the spring and summer months.

But the inclusion of dancing on church holy days worried the clergy, who said that it resulted in "unclene kyssynges" and "other unhonest handelynges." Indeed, Morris dancing *(below)* and traveling puppet shows *(above)* did include elements of ancient pagan rites, linking them irrefutably, in the eyes of some, with the work of the devil.

Marriage consumed everybody's attention in those days. Viewed as a business deal, marriage was arranged by thoughtful parents to ensure their children's—and the family's—prosperity and advancement. It was the precondition for, not the result of, love. William Paston's wife, Agnes, evidently thought so. A determined and quarrelsome woman who grew worse with age (and she lived to be nearly 80), she made her daughter Elizabeth's life miserable from the time the girl was 20. First she insisted that Elizabeth marry a 50-year-old man who said himself that he was disfigured by disease; when Elizabeth refused, the mother locked her in her room for three months. According to a cousin's letter, Elizabeth was "beaten once or twice a day, and sometimes thrice a day, and her head has been cut in two or three places."

Eventually, Elizabeth gave in, only to have the deal fall through. When Agnes did finally marry Elizabeth off, the bride's reaction to her betrothed seemed unenthusiastic, "My master, my best beloved as you call him, and I must needs call him so now," she wrote to her mother, "is full kind to me, and is as busy as he can to make me sure of my jointure," or wedding settlement.

The marriage of Agnes Paston's son John, however, was a distinct success. For in Margaret Mauteby, the child of an important Norfolk landowner, the matchmaking mother had found the perfect daughter-in-law. Things went well from the start, as Agnes reported in a letter to her husband in London shortly after Easter in 1440: "And as for the first acquaintance between John Paston and the said gentlewoman, she made him gentle cheer in gentle wise and said he was verily your son. And so I hope there shall need no great treaty between them." The negotiations went smoothly, and the young couple was married soon afterward.

Firm partners for 26 years, Margaret and John Paston grew to care deeply about one another, even though much of the time John was in London on the family's interminable legal business. But it is in her letters to her "right reverend and worshipful husband" that Margaret's feelings show.

"Please wear the ring with the image of St Margaret that I sent you as a keepsake until you come home," she wrote to John when she was pregnant with the first of their eight children. "You have left me such a keepsake as makes me think of you both day and night when I want to sleep." When he was ill, she fretted, begging him to return so that she could take care of him and promising a pilgrimage to two different shrines for his recovery.

Some marriages were performed by clergy, but many more were celebrated privately—with a ring, a promise, and an exchange of dowry.

John's letters to Margaret tended to be more businesslike and reserved. But after his wife had paid him what was obviously a happy visit in London, he addressed her romantically as "my own dear sovereign lady," and ended his letter with a homemade verse: "My Lord Percy and all this house / Recommend them to you, dog, cat and mouse / And wish that you had stayed a while / For they say you're a good girl."

At the time of Margaret's visit, the Pastons had been married for 24 years, and John had good reason to praise his wife. For with the help of her steward, Richard Calle, Margaret supervised a vast range of houses and manorial properties throughout Norfolk. She looked after her own breweries, bakehouses, dairies, and kitchens; what was not produced on the manors she bought in the county seat of Norwich or commissioned her husband to buy in London: pepper, cloves, ginger, cinnamon, almonds, dates, oranges. There are constant mentions of the stores that she was arranging. This was a huge job in itself, as household book listings of the period show. One August notation includes, "wheat baked, 8 quarters, 4 bushels; wine; barley and drage malt brewed, 18 quarters; beef, 2 carcasses, 3 quarters; pork, 5 pigs and 1 quarter;

Consanguinity charts like this one determined the marriageability of partners by their kinship ties.

1 young pig; 22 carcasses of mutton; 2 lambs; 1 capon; 333 pigeons; 1 heron; 460 white herrings; 18 salt fish; 6 stockfish."

In addition to the food there were other concerns—fabric, carefully described to her husband with instructions for prices to pay, was needed to make clothing, and all the furnishings of the houses, such as feather beds and bolsters, canopies and curtains, chests and bedsteads, had to be made or purchased.

But the Paston properties soon aroused the envy of the local nobility, who felt that they had been suffering under the new order. The family had to be constantly watchful.

And with John in London as often as he was, Margaret had to act in his stead; her letters are full of warnings about enemies' moves, negotiations with tenants, and court actions.

In October 1448, while John was away on business, a certain Lord Moleyns threatened to seize one of the Paston houses in a town called Gresham, about 20 miles north of Norwich. Margaret wrote urgently to her husband, asking for "some crossbows, and windlasses to wind them with, and crossbow bolts," as well as "two or three short pole-axes" to defend the property. But the weapons were not enough. For in January of the next year Moleyns sent a thousand men against the Gresham property. Armed with "knives, bows, arrows, shields, guns, pans with fire and burning tinder in them, long crowbars for pulling down houses, ladders, pickaxes," and other weapons, this force advanced on a building that Margaret was defending with about a dozen people. In short order, the lord's men drove everyone out, stole everything in the house, then tore it down.

Moleyns's action marked a real escalation of hostilities in Norfolk. But to his credit, John Paston managed to resolve the case by negotiation. Moreover, he acquired a powerful protector in Sir John Fastolf, who may have been one of Margaret's cousins.

Fastolf's reputation would suffer for centuries, after William Shakespeare turned him into the great comic character John Falstaff. The truth, however, is that Fastolf had had a long, distinguished, and extremely profitable career as a professional soldier—he was a Knight of the Garter—and when he retired home to Norfolk in the 1440s he owned at least 90 manors. But even in retirement he remained active, building a castle for himself at Caister on the North Sea coast. The scale of the castle's construction was magnificent, requiring a half dozen ships just to bring in the building materials. Towered and fortified, it covered six full acres, a treasure house of furniture, gold and silver plate, jewels, tapestries, and books. And besides its state rooms, chapel, and offices, it had 26 bedrooms, perhaps somewhat excessive for a man who was a childless widower.

All during this time of Fastolf's retirement, John Paston, whom the old man called "his heartiest kinsman and friend," served as his lawyer. And when the old knight died in 1459—at the amazing age of 78—he left everything to John.

By now the Pastons were among the richest people in the region. But their lands and properties—especially Caister, which Margaret called the fairest flower in their garland—were still attracting envy. With England in the grips of the dynastic Wars of the Roses, several powerful nobles felt emboldened to take what they wanted, backed as they were by their own private armies.

John Paston had no private army. But he did have influential friends in high places, and he knew how to use his family's favorite weapon, the law. While possession of Caister flew back and forth between the Pastons and their enemies, he and Margaret saw to it that their children were prepared to fight, too. This they did by training their sons in the law, by placing both sons and daughters with royal or noble patrons, and by arranging marriages.

The Pastons' first two sons—both named John, both lawyers, both knighted, and both members of parliament at Westminster—were as different as they could be. John-the-older's relations with his father were often tense. Things got so bad at the end of 1463, in fact, that the father even exiled his son to one of the family manors. Seeking to improve things between the pair, Margaret urged the boy to write to his father, "as humbly as you can, asking for his favour, and sending him such news as there is from where you are; and you should be careful of your spending, more so than you have been up till now, and live within your means, I am sure that you will find this the best way." And to her husband she wrote, "I beg you to take him back into favour, because I hope he is chastised and will be more careful after this."

Thanks to Margaret's efforts, the two men were eventually reconciled. But when his father died in 1466 and John became head of the family, the son's old thriftless ways returned. He wanted to live in splendor at Caister eventually, but for now he preferred the indulgences of the capital—fine clothes, betting, and tournaments—to the dreary legal battles for the Paston property.

John-the-older was a ladies' man, too. But although he kept a mistress, he never increased the family's power by marrying. This was another great disappointment to his mother. For in addition to her many other business concerns, Margaret was always involved in making good matches for her children.

If Margaret Paston may have given up on the older brother,

she worked for years on behalf of John-the-younger. The boy was a real concern. Responsible and hardworking, he was also amorous, and he badly wanted a suitable wife. In the end, though, he made a love match, albeit one that was suitably profitable: When he first met a young woman named Margery Brews, the daughter of a good Norfolk family, the two fell in love.

Still, bargaining over the marriage settlement was complicated. As to her mother's efforts to provide an adequate dowry, Margery wrote John, "she can get no more than you know of, which God knows, I am very sorry about. But if you love me, as I hope indeed that you do, you will not leave me because of it; if you did not have half the estates you have, I would not forsake you, even if I had to work as hard as any woman alive." Her entreaties must have worked. Pressed by her son, Margaret called the

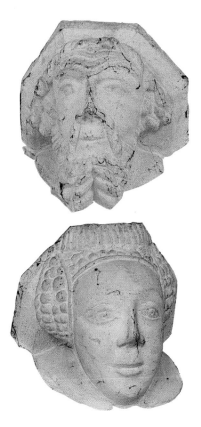

Found within the chancel of a 500-year-old church near Norwich, England, these stone heads are thought to be the only true-to-life representations of "Squire John Paston and his lady." The family tree at right chronicles the lineage of Paston's wife, Margaret Mauteby, up until their marriage in 1440.

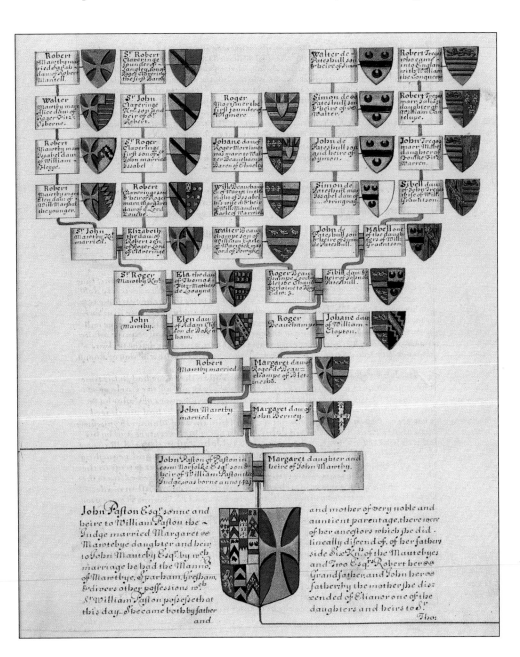

negotiating parties together, and the happy marriage was made.

But Margaret had less success with her elder daughter, also called Margery, who made a love match, too—in her case, with the family's steward, Richard Calle. When Margery told her mother that she and Calle had already exchanged vows in secret, Margaret, worthy daughter-in-law of Agnes Paston (who was still alive, and very much involved), sequestered her daughter and kept the pair apart for more than two years. She had no intention of allowing one of her children to marry a mere servant.

Eventually, Margaret had the bishop of Norwich examine the couple to see whether the words were binding; they were. The daughter was determined that the marriage should stand. As Margaret reported to John-the-older, "she repeated what she had said, and boldly said that if these words did not make things sure, she would make it sure

thing else. This she managed to do for the 18 years that she survived her husband, anxiously seeing her family through every swing of war and fortune.

Eventually the battles with the contenders over Fastolf's estate were settled. And while the Pastons lost a portion of their inheritance, Margaret's son John-the-older did at last peacefully take up residence at Caister Castle. "Blessed be God," he wrote to his younger brother and namesake, "I have Caister as I want it." When he died, unmarried and without an heir, Margery and John-the-younger took over the remaining Paston properties, and during the more stable reigns of the Tudors and the Stuarts, the family prospered even further. Indeed, their wealth would become proverbial throughout Norfolk and the surrounding country: "There was never a Paston poor, a Heydon a coward, or a Cornwallis a fool."

"There was never a Paston poor, a Heydon a coward, or a Cornwallis a fool."

before she left; for she said that she thought she was bound in conscience, whatever the words were. These foolish words grieve me and her grandmother as much as everything else together."

Margaret could not change the binding words, but she would not tolerate the disobedience. When Margery came to visit her mother in Norwich, her mother had her turned away from the door. "We have only lost a good-for-nothing in her," she told John-the-older, spitefully. "You can be sure that she will regret her foolishness afterwards, and I pray to God that she does."

Over the years Margaret and Margery seem to have settled their differences. As far as Margaret was concerned, keeping the Pastons united and prosperous was more important than any-

Unlike her youth, Margaret Paston's old age was a time of peace, with the family comfortably rich and the grandchildren growing. In her will she carefully left bequests to all of her children and grandchildren (including an illegitimate child fathered by John-the-older and a son born to her daughter Margery Calle), to her friends and servants, and to the church. Margaret had made full arrangements for her funeral as well as for her tomb, and when she passed away in November 1484, she was buried within sight of the towers of Caister Castle. On her gravestone were etched two coats of arms: those of her own family, the Mautebys, and the ones that were created specially for the Pastons after they had risen from the peasantry to achieve wealth and honors.

A Child's World

"Children often have bad habits, and think only of the present, ignoring the future. . . . They cry and weep more over the loss of an apple than over the loss of an inheritance. . . . They desire everything they see, and call and reach for it. . . . Suddenly they laugh, suddenly they weep, and are continuously yelling, chattering, and laughing."

- Bartholomew the Englishman, 13th-century monk

Childbirth and Infancy

In medieval times childbirth could be a time of either great joy or great sorrow. Mortality rates for both mother and baby were high, and many children who lived through the birth died shortly thereafter. During the delivery, some peasant women received help from female neighbors; others could rely only on their husbands. A woman of the merchant or noble classes was attended by midwives and female relatives. The chamber would be dimly lit, and a warm bath prepared for the infant *(below)*; both measures were designed to ease the transition from the womb into the world. The expectant father performed the important job of appealing to the saints for the safety of his wife and child.

The infant was wrapped in swaddling clothes—long cloths wrapped around the body and secured with crisscross bands. Swaddling kept the child warm but was also said to force the limbs to grow straight. Unless work prevented it, peasants and artisans nursed their own babies, but wealthy mothers hired other women to serve as wet nurses. Without the burden of nursing, which can serve as a natural birth control, such women sometimes conceived as frequently as biologically possible, bearing as many as 20 children.

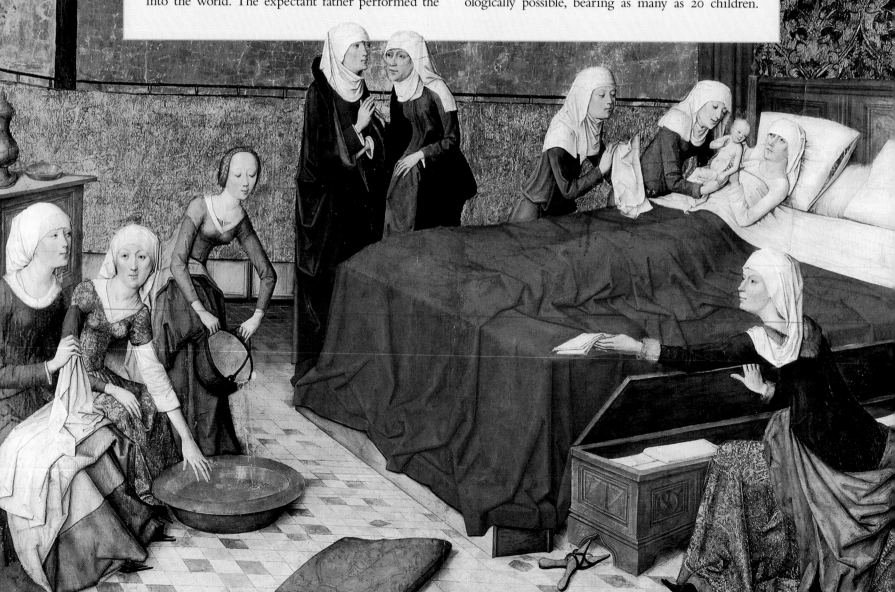

A Cesarean section saves the
life of a child whose mother has
died during labor *(right).* Midwives were told to ask a man to
make the incision if they lacked
the courage to do it themselves.

Some babies slumbered cozily
in cradles, such as this 500-
year-old wooden one from
England *(below),* but many
more slept with family members or with wet nurses.

Death stalks an infant as a mother
looks on helplessly. About 50 to
60 percent of children never saw
their fifth birthday.

Time for Play

Parents, preachers, and philosophers all agreed with medieval author Philip of Novare that "children should be allowed to play since nature demands it." And although parents were counseled to use strict discipline and Christian morality to guide their children, most felt that children younger than seven were not really capable of learning lessons or telling good from evil. So the first years of a child's life were generally free of the burdens of formal education or hard work.

As always, children enjoyed playing outdoors, fashioning mills and dams out of water, earth, and sticks or building houses and castles from sand; one observer said that future saints built sand churches. Group games, such as hide-and-seek, ballgames, and winter snowball fights *(below),* were popular, and younger children learned the rules by imitating their older brothers and sisters. Children used their imaginations to transform blocks of wood into knights, sticks into horses or swords, and pieces of bread into boats. Some were lucky enough to have a toy crafted solely for play: Spinning tops, miniature windmills, rocking horses, balls, hoops, dolls, whistles, and clay birds made up the medieval child's realm of playthings.

The peasant boy at far right is enjoying one of the side benefits of the November pig slaughter: a pig bladder blown up into a balloon. In summer these balloons served as children's water wings.

Riding a hobby horse, the lad at left waves a lance with windmill blades at his brother, who is learning to get around using a wheeled walker.

A well-used ceramic doll *(right)* and a battle-scarred wooden sword *(above)* show evidence of serious play. Girls also played with miniature cooking utensils.

Time for Work

When children reached the age of seven, their parents swiftly set them on the path toward their future livelihoods. For a privileged few that meant formal education, but the vast majority of children learned a trade or went to work as farm laborers or servants. Opportunities for each child were limited both by social status and by gender. A girl of the upper class, for example, was taught reading and mathematics, but just enough so that she might successfully manage a household of servants and its accounts; the remainder of her training, as for her poorer counterparts, involved spinning, weaving, and other domestic arts *(below, left)*.

Most peasant girls and boys never learned to read or write. From a young age they helped with the farm work, hauled water to laborers, or tended the livestock and younger siblings. Children of lesser means in urban society also received little in the way of schooling, getting their job training from apprenticeships with skilled artisans or craftsmen. Boys from prosperous families also served as apprentices, but they were taught banking, commerce, and the law.

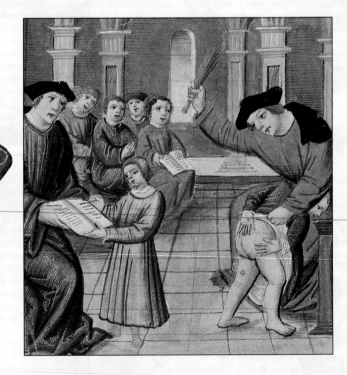

A teacher applies his cane to the backside of a disobedient pupil in a French elementary school, where students learned hymns, letters, grammar, rhetoric, and arithmetic.

CHAPTER FOUR

Of Towns and Tradesmen

Tempted by the wares and services that are offered by a variety of shops—those of a tailor, furrier, barber, and grocer—two Parisians make their way along one of the city's paved streets. As cities grew, village marketplaces evolved into large commercial districts where artisans plied their trades in storefronts to attract customers.

 hen Alexander Neckam rode into Paris, he was astonished by the sheer press of human activity all around him. Neckam was a budding scholar who had led a sheltered life in the sedate English provinces. He had never seen any place like Paris, which in the late 1170s was the largest city in the Western world. With a population of perhaps 50,000 inhabitants, it was five times the size of London.

In those days of cramped, ill-lit dwellings, urban life in every European city was lived very much in the street. Shops opened onto the roadway like stalls in an oriental bazaar. All manner of artisans and craftsmen—carpenters and cobblers, tailors and tanners—plied their trade in the open air for all to see. Housewives gossiped by public fountains and children improvised games, fashioning playgrounds out of every empty lot and back alley.

In Paris it was the same, only more so. An endless procession of humans and animals clogged the rutted, unpaved thoroughfares—peasant women hurrying to market with baskets of fruit; herders steering flocks of bleating, jittery sheep; teamsters shouting oaths at obstinate mules. For Neckam, a young man of 20 and more used to the calm of the cloister, it was a rollicking scene.

Students used a tablet held like a hand mirror to memorize the alphabet. Instructors expected their pupils to recite the letters after one week's study.

Parents hand over their son and a bag of gold for his support to the abbot of the local monastery. Throughout much of the Middle Ages, parents could make a binding monastic vow for their children.

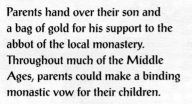

A peasant boy lends a hand with the grain at harvesttime. Boys and girls helped their families by gleaning fields, picking wild fruit and berries, and gathering firewood.

CLEANING UP

As more and more people left the countryside and moved into towns and cities, waste disposal and public hygiene in the increasingly congested areas became major concerns. Sewage and animal cadavers were thrown into the rivers; butchers let the blood of slaughtered animals flow into the gutters, as did dyers the contaminated water from their vats. From fishmongers' shops like the one at left, unsold fish were tossed into the street at the end of the day.

For the most part municipal hygiene laws did little to prevent these practices, and those citizens who, like the man below wearing clogs to stay above the muck, tried to sweep up the accumulated refuse often had to compete with the free-roaming pigs that rooted in the garbage. Some towns tried to restrict the activities of porcine scavengers, imposing a fine on owners who let their pigs run free on a Sunday—and an even higher fine if the offending animal was a sow.

From dawn to dusk, the streets hummed with activity, while in the numerous taverns with their huge wine casks, long benches, and reed-strewn floors, drinkers with nothing better to do spent their time gambling on dice games. There was open-air entertainment, too, for those who had time to watch it. Clowns bumped and tumbled, jugglers showed off their skills, and minstrels crooned the latest ballads to the accompaniment of a fiddlelike instrument called the vielle.

Roving troupes of actors performed morality tales for the crowds, often enlivening popular Bible stories with slapstick comedy and satirical asides to the audience. And behind this incessant hustle and bustle, church bells tolled away the hours, dictating the rhythm of people's lives across the city—for in the perpetual half-light of the narrow streets, the passage of time was heard rather than seen.

Paris also had a less appealing side. The city's poorer residents lived crammed into fetid hovels. There were open drains and ditches, no streetlights, no sidewalks, and for the most part no paving in the streets except in a few major thoroughfares laid down in the style of the Romans who had settled there more than a thousand years before. Parisians had to negotiate marshy pools whenever there was rain.

Sewage disposal was a particular problem, with most of the runoff finding its way into the river Seine. Garbage often ended up in the streets, where dogs and pigs scavenged among the scraps. So too, sometimes, did human wastes. King Louis IX himself was once doused with the contents of a chamber pot emptied thoughtlessly from an upstairs window.

And if monks and lawyers and tradesmen and scholars crowded the streets, so too did less desirable citizens. Beggars slumped listlessly outside of the churches or solicited alms by showing off running sores or the stumps of severed limbs. Thieves moved through the crowds with studied nonchalance, looking for a well-stuffed purse that could be cut loose from the belt with a quick lunge of the knife. Retribution was also there for all to see. Unfailingly, the Paris gallows displayed a crop of 24 decomposing corpses; each time a fresh criminal was executed, one was cut down in order to make room for the new arrival.

In its vitality and its squalor, Paris was typical of the urban centers that were burgeoning all across Europe between the 11th and 13th centuries. This was a time when trade was recovering from the shock of the Viking raids and

A Flemish couple assist customers in their jewelry shop in this 14th-century illumination. Women frequently took part in family businesses, from working in the shop to bookkeeping; some even carried on their husband's trade after his death. In the foreground, a monkey—a symbol of human vanity—taunts a dog with a bone.

when a new prosperity was spreading across the continent from the ports of northern Italy and Flanders, where a busy maritime traffic oiled the wheels of commerce. But even far inland, sleepy villages that happened to find themselves on major trade routes blossomed into walled cities, while buyers and sellers from every point of the compass flocked to huge annual fairs. In the half-century from 1150 to 1200 alone, the number of chartered cities in the Holy Roman Empire more than tripled, from 200 to over 600.

There were many reasons for this urban explosion, most of which had to do with trade. From the 10th century on, the population of the continent began to grow rapidly, creating a class of landless laborers who could find no place for themselves in the rigid economy of the feudal estates. Many took to the roads as peddlers, carrying their wares on their backs and earning a precarious living by providing peasants and landowners with the few goods they needed that could not be produced locally.

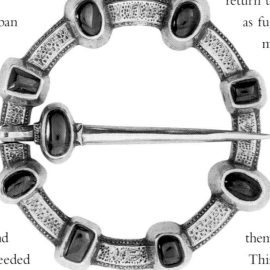

The alternating rubies and sapphires in this 13th-century gold brooch were polished by "bruting," rubbing two stones together to give each a rounded shape.

The more enterprising of the peddlers quickly realized that there were big profits to be made in buying commodities where they were plentiful and cheap, and selling them where they were rare. The process involved travel, for the farther the wares were taken from their source, the better the price they fetched. And so a whole new class of long-distance merchants developed. "Piepowders" they were called, from the French *pieds poudreux*—literally, "dusty footed."

They were a hardy and courageous breed, these early merchant-adventurers, all too accustomed to the bone-jarring discomfort of rides on horse- or mule-back over rugged roads as well as long hikes on foot through all kinds of weather. Rivers had to be forded and forests traversed. Brigands waited to way-lay them by land and pirates by sea. In remote parts they even faced the threat of attack by wolves and other wild animals.

Yet the rewards could be great. Before long the more successful had amassed large sums of money. They needed a place to store their wealth and a base to retire to in the winter months when the roads were impassable. Most could not return to their homelands for fear of being seized as fugitive serfs. Instead they headed for communities on the trade routes where other merchants gathered.

Often these merchants' quarters were established inside fortified settlements, but in other places they grew up outside the walls. These were the original suburbs, literally *sub urbe,* Latin for "beneath the city." Before long, though, enough wealth was accumulated for them to afford walls of their own.

This coming together of merchants also affected the way in which the traders did business. Only too aware of the dangers of long-distance commerce, they started forming partnerships to share the rewards and spread the risk. Typically, one merchant would put up capital to buy trading goods while another would take responsibility for the voyage. This led to the formation of companies in which merchants agreed to cooperate for a number of journeys over a limited period of time—say, two or three years.

With the spread of joint enterprise, a new, rooted merchant class appeared. Such men no longer personally faced the risks of the open road. Instead they put up their money, then waited behind town walls for the profits to roll in. And return they did,

Plague victims sought help wherever they could find it: The stricken family at left relies on the prayers of a priest; others turned to so-called Beak Doctors *(below)*, medical men who wore bird masks in order to protect themselves from infection.

wife," observed Italian author Giovanni Boccaccio. "Nay what is more . . . , fathers and mothers were found to abandon their own children."

The toll was terrible. In the countryside so many peasants perished that the manorial system itself was threatened. But things were even worse in the cities, where overcrowded conditions and poor sanitation were ideal incubators for disease. In some urban areas as many as 600 people died each day. Londoners buried corpses in mass graves six feet deep, six feet wide, and 100 yards long. And in Milan living and dead might share the same fate: All members of a victim's household were walled up together to die.

Perhaps the worst natural disaster Europe had ever seen, the plague abated and recurred, seeming to run its dreadful course only to strike again. The Black Death of 1347 subsided in 1351, but another epidemic followed in 1361, another in 1369, and another every decade for the rest of the century. Its ultimate disappearance remains a mystery.

Medicine proved powerless to stop it, and academia was at a loss to explain it. Into this void flooded a host of wild theories. Some blamed the Jews for poisoning the water supply; others, the sinister conjunction of the planets Saturn, Jupiter, and Mars; still others, "corrupt vapors." Some even suggested that the plague was passed on through "lust with old women."

But most believed that the Black Death was God's vengeance on sinful man. "So many died that all believed it was the end of the world," remembered Siena's Agnolo di Tura, who lost five of his children to the plague. So widespread was this sense of resignation, wrote di Tura, that after a time "no one wept for any death, for all awaited death."

Some wealthy people hoped crucifix-adorned amulets *(right)* would keep them safe; others, like the citizens of Florence shown below, fled the city for the healthier air of the countryside.

. . . And in the same hour [my wife] Antonia was sick to death, and in the same bed with her the second boy, who died beside her. Imagine how my heart broke, as I heard the little ones weeping, and their mother not strong. . . . Think of it: three dead!"

Yet even in those dark times, some individuals managed to prosper. The recipient of that letter, a merchant by the name of Francesco di Marco Datini, happened to be among them. He was one of the 14th-century's self-made men, building up a business empire through unflagging effort and ceaseless attention to detail.

The son of a poor tavern keeper, Datini, too, knew all about the plague; he lost his entire family, with the exception of one brother, in the original outbreak. Burdened with this sorrow, he set off alone as a 15-year-old in 1350 to seek his fortune in Avignon, where the pope had taken up residence 45 years before. Scraping together the sum of 150 florins from the sale of a small piece of land, he set himself up in business. Soon he was running a luxury-goods store near the papal palace, selling everything from arms and armor to silks and Spanish leather. The shop prospered, and by the time he finally decided to return to his hometown of Prato in northern Italy 32 years later, he had increased his wealth more than twentyfold.

He took a wife with him. Margherita was 25 years his junior

and of noble birth, though the family had lost everything when her father was executed in the course of a Florentine civil war. Francesco accepted her without a dowry—an unusual act for a canny businessman, suggesting the union was, at least on his part, a love match.

Back in Prato, Francesco built a splendid mansion that stands to this day. He also expanded his business empire into Spain and the Balearic Islands. Much of his time was spent at the head office in Florence, forcing him to communicate with Margherita, 15 miles away in Prato, by letter.

He was a tireless correspondent, as he was the first to recognize: "I am not feeling very well today," he wrote when he was over 60, "on account of all the writing I have done in these two days, without sleeping either by night or by day, and in these two days eating but one loaf." He was also a compulsive hoarder who—fortunately for history—never threw away any of his papers. Sometime after his death the entire heap of 150,000 letters and business records was sealed up in a dusty recess under the stairs of his Prato home. Four and a half centuries later, in 1870, renovators discovered the trove, bringing to light the intimate details of Francesco and Margherita's married life.

It was not an easy match; Margherita was a spirited young woman who had to cope with the ceaseless nagging of a cranky, workaholic husband. At first his communications adopted a patronizing tone, but she would have none of it. When he wrote that one of her letters must have been dictated because it seemed "beyond the fashion of a young female," it was too much for her

pride to bear. "I have a little of the Gherardini blood, though I prize it not overmuch," she wrote imperiously, pointedly drawing attention to her own superior breeding, "but what *your* blood is, I know not."

It was typical of well-to-do 14th-century ladies to give much time and attention to their wardrobe, and Margherita was no exception. She devoted much space in her letters to Francesco to the subject of fabric, which her husband would dutifully procure and ship to her to be made into garments under her direct supervision. One time she complained that the material he had sent had shrunk before cutting, leaving too little for a complete ensemble. "So see to it," she admonished Francesco, "if there is no way of getting me a little more for the *cappuccio* [hood], for I should not like to have a new cloak with an old cappuccio."

As befitting the wife of an affluent merchant, Margherita possessed gowns of the finest silk, velvet, and damask in a rainbow of vibrant colors. In the style of the day, dresses reached to the floor, and sometimes stretched out behind in a long train. The sleeves were very elaborate and detachable—Margherita had sleeves of vermilion velvet, and squirrel and rabbit fur—to be mixed and matched with different gowns.

These fashions raised the ire of some menfolk. "What doth a woman's train stir up when she walks in the road?" fussed one. "Dust—and in the winter it wallows in the mud. And the person who walks behind her in summer breathes the incense she has stirred up . . . And lo! in winter she muddies herself and spoils her garments at the hem. . . . And if she sets the maid to

"I have resolved to go not only to Pisa, but to the world's end, as it please you."

THE RISE OF BANKING

The currencies of Italy's merchant cities were among the most stable in medieval Europe. The banking industry first thrived there, developing such techniques of modern business as double-entry bookkeeping and prices based on supply and demand.

The two scenes at left show Italian bankers at work—counting their coins on the benches, or banks, from which they took their name *(top),* and entering accounts while customers wait to be served *(bottom).* Among the currencies that would have passed through their hands was Florence's florin, shown below, a coin widely accepted in international business.

clean it, how loudly she swears, wishing at the devil the sow, her lady!" And of the "sleeves or rather sacks," the writer Franco Sacchetti observed, "What more foolish, inconvenient and useless fashion has there ever been? For none can take up a glass or a mouthful from the table, without soiling her sleeve or the cloth, with the glasses she has overturned."

Despite the occasional disparagement, Margherita seemed to have been well pleased with her wardrobe, and her husband, perhaps to make up for his other shortcomings, continued to indulge her expensive habits. In other areas of their relationship, odd references in letters suggest that the marriage remained stormy, yet not totally devoid of affection.

At one point, when business dealings forced Francesco to linger in Pisa for an extended period, he asked his wife to join him—in his customary grumpy manner: "I eat naught that pleases me, and they are not things to my liking, and the bowls are coarse. Were you here, I would be more at ease." On this occasion, Margherita's reply was softer and more gentle-hearted: "Meseems it would please you to have me there with the whole household, and yet you leave the choice to me. This you do of your courtesy, and I am not worthy of so much honour. I have resolved to go not only to Pisa, but to the world's end, as it please you."

And yet for some unknown reason, Margherita did not join her husband in Pisa. Their separations—ostensibly for business reasons—continued, and their correspondence grew more acrimonious. "You are not wont to bring me too many gifts when you come home," she noted sourly in one letter. In another, she stood up for herself stoutly, "And I am in the right, and you will not change it by shouting!" Sometimes, her outbursts elicited a contrite reply from Francesco. "It has pleased God to soften my heart about many things which used to grieve you—and you were right, and I never said you were not."

But her most bitter reproach came after Francesco had compared her unfavorably with the wife of a mutual friend. "He keeps his wife as a woman and not as an innkeeper's wife!" she replied indignantly, no doubt thinking of her husband's constant arrivals and departures. She went on to compare his treatment of her with that he meted out to a favorite mule, "to whom you have given so much to eat and so much ease that she was about to burst. Would God you treated me as well!"

The overriding cause of friction in their marriage was that Margherita failed to provide Datini with the one thing he most wanted—an heir. As the years passed, with Margherita still seemingly unable to conceive, the tension between them grew. Nosy friends and well-meaning relatives offered an abundance of dubiously helpful advice. Margherita's sister wrote from Florence, "Many women here are with child . . . I went to inquire and found out the remedy they have used: a poultice, which they put on their bellies." She added, however, that the poultice, "stinks so much, that there have been husbands who have thrown it away. So discover from Francesco if he would have you wear it. . . . And may God and the Virgin Mary and the blessed St. John the Baptist grant you this grace."

It is not recorded whether the couple employed this home prescription—though the poultice's stench would seem counter-productive to the task at hand. In any event, Margherita remained childless and, aware of her husband's disappointment, she grew jealous, constantly suspecting him of infidelities. "I believe no word you write. On every other matter I would take my oath that you would never tell a lie; but . . . as to this I would vow that you never spoke the truth."

As it turned out, she had good reason to be suspicious; in his desperate desire for an heir—even an illegitimate one—the aging Francesco committed indiscretions that were increasingly obvious to those around him. His brother-in-law wrote to him, "Greet Margherita for me, and when you leave for Pisa, tell her from me to remind you of what the women of the Marches say to their husbands at parting: 'Remember your home!' And she will understand me well."

Finally, it was a slave in Francesco and Margherita's own household who bore Datini a daughter, named Ginevra. At first Margherita would not have the baby in the house. A document

A rendering of the exterior of the Datinis' home in Prato, northern Italy, shows the frescoes that depicted Francesco's life story. The paintings were done by the merchant's fellow citizens after his death, an honor usually reserved for princes and popes.

refers to her as "a certain girl who was secretly placed in the hospital of S. Maria Nuova." Soon, she was installed with a family and regular payments were made "to the husband of the foster mother who keeps Francesco's daughter."

But six years later, when Margherita had perhaps at last given up hope of having a child of her own, she changed her mind and welcomed Ginevra into the family. "Vex yourself not about Ginevra," she wrote of the girl to her husband, "but be assured that I look to her as if she were my own, as indeed I consider

her." Eventually Ginevra was provided with a handsome dowry and was married off to the young cousin of one of Datini's business partners.

As time passed, Margherita devoted increasing space in her letters to matters of religion, seeking to persuade her husband to turn his thoughts away from business and the secular world. "But assuredly, if you alter not your manner of life and give up a few things of this world, and look to your soul as well as your body, I fear all will turn against us." She was undoubtedly pleased, then,

Two masons lay stone for a tower while laborers raise a scaffold around the building and others lift a block of stone with a wheel-operated crane. In addition to working at the construction site, a master mason acted as architect, contractor, and engineer. Some masons were also sculptors, like Anton Pilgram of Vienna (above), whose self-portrait appears on the pulpit of the city's cathedral.

when he finally decided to make his peace with God by leaving all his wealth to a foundation set up to help Prato's poor. She herself received a house, land, and furnishings, plus an annuity of 100 gold florins a year for as long as she remained a widow. She survived her husband by 13 years, spending much of that time in the Florentine home of her adopted daughter.

Margherita's devotion to her faith was characteristic of her time and place in history. For in spite of the indignities of the Avignon exile and the Great Schism, faith remained at the core of medieval life, a firm bedrock of belief on which townspeople and country dwellers alike built their deepest hopes and fears.

And the outward signs of their devotion were everywhere to be seen. The epoch's greatest legacy remains the amazing profusion of churches scattered in towns and villages across the continent. The sheer scale of the enterprise was extraordinary. Between the mid-11th and mid-14th centuries, 80 cathedrals and 500 large churches were built in France alone. By 1350 more stone had been quarried for their construction than for all the pyramids of Egypt.

They were built for the most part by architect-engineers who personally supervised large teams of workers—more than a thousand in the case of cathedrals—who came from the guilds and lived in "lodges" near the construction site. The carpenters, metalworkers, and painters who contributed so much to the splendor of these buildings did so for the most part anonymously; they were regarded as artisans rather than artists.

The relationship between employer and worker was not always a happy one, as records of the preparation of choir stalls for the cathedral at Rouen in France show. Delicate workmanship was needed, for the bottom of each folding seat was decorated with a carving known as a misericord. These flat-topped projections, some in the form of gargoylelike grotesques and others depicting scenes of everyday life, were meant to serve as supports for weary choristers to rest against during lengthy church services.

The man chosen by the cathedral chapter to oversee the work was a master carpenter named Philippot Viart. He recruited about a dozen craftsmen, and a house belonging to the church's dean was rented for his use. Viart moved in with his family; the building was to be both his workshop and his home for as long as the assignment lasted.

At first the job went well. A commission examined the first set of seats and pronounced them acceptable—as well it might, for these stalls were long regarded as masterpieces of the carvers' art. But work of such high standards took time. As first months and then years dragged by, the chapter grew increasingly concerned about the slowness with which the work was progressing and hired more carpenters.

Eventually, after nine years, they decided enough was enough. They set a deadline for the stalls to be completed. Viart and his men missed it. Six months later, the chapter retaliated by sacking most of the carpenters, keeping on only Viart and one other worker. When fresh craftsmen were drafted from the surrounding region, the chapter took care to employ them on a piecework basis rather than at a daily rate.

Viart himself did not long survive under the new regime. Three months later he was served with notice of eviction from the house and was threatened with the confiscation of his possessions and imprisonment. There is no record of these punishments being carried out, so it seems that, after over a decade on the job, he finally agreed to go peacefully.

It is impossible to tell how many similar stories marked the creation of Europe's matchless endowment of religious buildings. No doubt there were many such disputes, for no great enterprise is ever achieved without pain. Time has erased the human cost of the venture, leaving only the serene achievement itself for future ages to contemplate. But behind the silent stones lies a vivid, troubled, yet endlessly creative, world.

Cathedrals: For the Glory of God

With its spires stretching toward the heavens, Chartres Cathedral dominates the surrounding French countryside, an eloquent symbol of the majesty and power of the Christian faith. Between the 12th and 16th centuries, many such cathedrals—later called Gothic, or barbaric, because their style was considered crude by the artists of the Renaissance—proliferated throughout Europe, a testament to the religious devotion of the men and women of the Middle Ages.

Construction of a cathedral often took over 100 years and required the efforts of every level of medieval society. The wealthy donated huge sums of money, the middle class provided skilled artisans, and peasants gave unskilled labor. The fervor of the times was such that those who could least afford it could be the most generous. It was said that one of the most glorious cathedrals, Notre Dame, was built with little more than the hard earned farthings donated by devout old women.

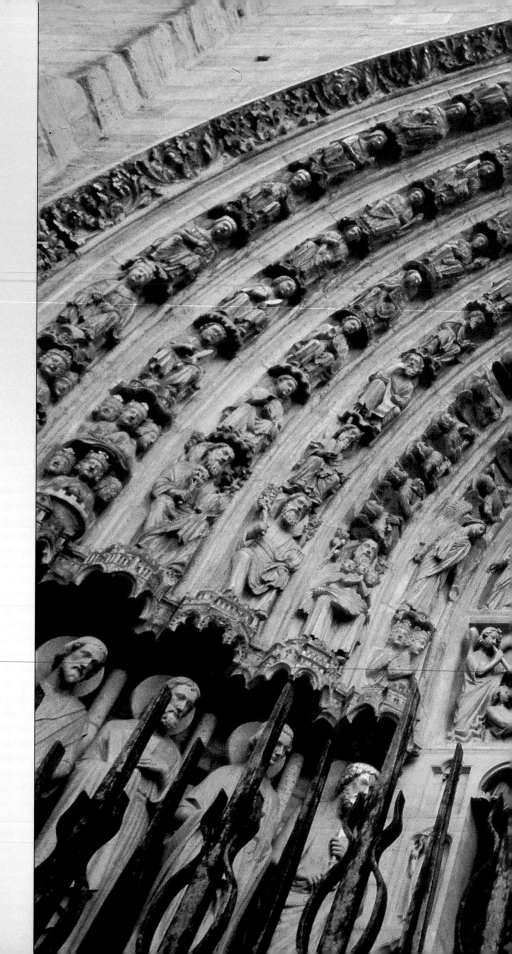

A cathedral's exterior decoration captures the imagination at first sight. The magnificent main portal of Notre Dame in Paris *(right)* tells the story of the New Testament in stone, while a gargoyle *(above)* surveys Paris from his lofty perch, as though searching for the demons that he was meant to repulse.

Showing the wear of seven centuries, the so-called Heavenly Stair of England's Wells Cathedral *(far left)* leads either to the gallery over the choir or to the cathedral's chapter house. Majestic inverted arches *(left),* although added to support its top-heavy central tower centuries after Wells was built, seem perfectly in tune with the cathedral's original plan.

Deceptively slender pillars support the soaring arches of the apse and nave of the French cathedral at Amiens, drawing the eye heavenward *(far left)*, where the ceiling's crossed ribs gracefully intersect *(left)*. A member of the celestial ensemble gracing the Pillar of the Angels in France's Strasbourg Cathedral *(above)* stands ready to sound the horn on Judgment Day.

Sunlight illuminates the south rose window of the cathedral at Chartres *(above)*, revealing the story of the Second Coming of Christ. Colored rays from stained-glass windows at Bourges Cathedral in France *(right)* bathe a stone pillar with an ethereal glow.

Great Schism: 136, 147
Grosseteste, Robert: *128*
Guilds: 129-133; Augsburg members take office, *132;* badges of, *133*
Gutenberg Bible: 11

H

Hallmoot: 98-99
Hamburg: *137*
Hamesucken *(hamsoken):* 99
Hanseatic League: *136-137*
Haut Koenigsburg Castle: *62*
Haywards: 98
Healing: *96-97;* and hospitals, *26;* and midwives, 114-*115;* and physicians, *96-97, 140*
Heavenly Stair (Wells Cathedral): *152*
Hedingham Castle: *63*
Hell: *28*
Heloise: 19, 29-33, 39-*41;* affair with Abelard, 29-31; marriage to Abelard, 33; quoted, 31, 33, 41
Henry (Young King): 66-68, 76
Henry I (king of England): 51, 54
Henry II (king of England): 10, 24, 55-58, *56,* 63-69, 76
Henry III (king of England): 77-78, 134
Henry III (king of Germany): 9
Henry V (king of England): 106
Heraldry: 76-77
Herbal medicines: *97*
Hildegard von Bingen (abbess and visionary): 9, 22-25, *23;* convents of, *22,* 24; quoted, 23; songs of, *25;* visions of, 22-23, *24-25*
Hobby horse: *117*
Horn, hunting: *60*
Hospitals: *26*
Houses: of laborers, 92; of villagers, 98; of lords, *61-63*
Humanism: 11
Hundred Years' War: 11, *50-51,* 100, 106, 136
Hunting: 59-60

I

Illuminated manuscripts: *18*
Imbolc (pagan feast): 104
Infant mortality: 114-*115*
Innocent II (pope): 38
Innocent III (pope): 83, 126

Irminon (abbot of Saint-Germain): 91, 92
Isabella of Bourbon: 52
Isabel of Striguil: 77

J

Jacoba of Hainault: *53*
James (saint): 34-*35*
Jerusalem: *84-87, 85*
Jewelry: *124, 125*
Joan of Arc (saint): 11, *100-102;* execution of, *102*
John (king of England): 69, 78; charter of, *135*
John of Brabant: *52*
John of Salisbury: 69
Jousting: 72-74
Jurors: 98-99
Jutta (Benedictine abbess): 22

K

Kitchens: 62; at Eltz Castle, *62*
Knights: 9, 53, 69-71, *70,* 76; on crusade, *82;* education of, 69-71; equipment of, 71, *73,* 74, *83;* in murder of Thomas Becket, 67, *68;* and tournaments, *72-75*
Knights Templar: 78

L

Laborers: children as, *118, 119;* in cities, 129; and court cases, 99; food of, 94, 103, 105; rebellion of, *95,* 99; tasks of, *91, 93*-95, 105; and dues paying, *94*
Lammas: 104
Laon, cathedral of: 10
Legal system: 98-99; benefit of clergy in, 63
Leo III (pope): 8, 10, *14,* 15-17
Literacy: 19, 27, 69, 118, 130-131
London: 134-136; plague in, 140
Longbows: *54*
Louis VII (king of France): 55, 69
Louis IX (king of France): 82, *83*
Love: courtly, 67; in marriage, 108-109, 112, 142
Lugnasadh (pagan feast): 104

M

Magna Carta: 11
Manorial system: 8, *88-89,* 89-112; courts of, 98-99; dues paying in, *94*
Manuscripts: *21, 130-131;* copied in

monasteries, *46;* illuminated, *18*
Margaret (wife of Young King, Henry): 76
Marriage: 67, 107-109, 112; ceremony, *108;* consanguinity charts, *109;* of the Datinis, 142, 144-146
Marshal, John: 51
Marshal, William: 51-52, 61, 69-78; arms of, 77
Mary of Burgundy: *53*
Matilda (queen of England): 51, 54-55
Maurus, Hrabanus (abbot of Fulda): 27
May Day: 104
Medicine. *See* Healing
Merchants: 10, *120-121,* 121-126, *124,* 139; and banking, *143;* Francesco di Marco Datini, 141-147; education of, 126; in urban power struggles, 134
Messina (Sicily), plague in, 139
Midsummer Night: 104
Midwives: 114-*115*
Monasteries: 9, 19, *42-49;* Canterbury, *43;* Cîteaux, 37; Clairvaux, 37; Cluny, 8, 37; corrupt, 37, 39; education in, 19, 22, 25, 118, 119; Fontevrault, *48-49;* Fulda, 19; hospitals run by, *26;* life in, 20-22, 25, 43-48, *44;* and literature, *46,* 130; Monreale, *44-45;* oblates to, 19-20, 37-38, *119;* reading in, *46;* Reichenau, 25; Royaumont, *46-47;* Rupertsberg, *22,* 24; Saint-Denis, 33, 38-40; Saint-Germain des Prés, 89-95; Saint-Gildas-de-Rhuys, 39; Saint Martin-du-Canigou, *42;* work in, *48*
Monks: corrupt, *38-39;* monastic life of, *42-49. See also* Monasteries
Montfort, Simon de: 134
Morris dancing: *107*
Muslims: 13; crusades and, 79, 84-87, *85, 86;* scientific legacy of, 128

N

Neckam, Alexander: 121, 126
Neck verses: 63
Neuillay manor: 89-95
Nomadic tribes: 13
Notre Dame Cathedral: 10, 126, 149, *150-151*

O

Oblates: 19-20, 37-38, *119*
Order of Saint Mary Magdalene: 129

P

Paraclete (convent): 39-40
Paris: *120-121,* 121-129; education in, 10, 126-128; University of, 10
Paston, Agnes Berry: 106-107; quoted, 108
Paston, Clement: 106
Paston, Elizabeth: 107
Paston, John (father): 108-110, *111;* quoted, 109
Paston, John (older son): 110, 112
Paston, John (younger son): 110-112
Paston, Margaret Mauteby: 106, 108-112, *111;* family tree of, *111;* quoted, 108-112
Paston, Margery (Calle): 112
Paston, Margery Brews: 111
Paston, William: 106-108
Patrick, earl of Salisbury: 75
Pentecost: 104
Philip II (king of France): 68, 77-78
Philip the Good: *53*
Philip of Novare: 116
Physicians: *96-97;* Beak Doctors, *140;* manuals for, *96-97*
Piepowders: 125
Pilgrimage: 34, 108; *map* 35
Pilgrim's Guide: 34-*35*
Pillar of the Angels (Strasbourg Cathedral): *155*
Plague: 11, 136-141; victims of, *138, 139, 140*
Play: *116, 117;* ball game, *106;* chess, *65*
Popes: 9-10, 55; Alexander III, 66; in Avignon, 136, 141, 147; choosing, 38; and Great Schism, 136, 147; Innocent II, 38; Innocent III, 83, 126; Leo III, 8, 10, *14,* 15-17; Urban II, 79, *80;* Urban III, 87
Priests: *30, 32-33;* corrupt, 37

Q

Quadrivium: 126

R

Reapers: 105

Reeve: 98-99
Reeve, Michael: 98-99
Relics: *31*
Religion: pagan, 89, 95, 103-105. *See also* Catholic Church
Renaissance: 11
Richard I (the Lion-Hearted; king of England): 10, 68, 76-78, 80, 126
Richard of Wallingford: *46*
Robert, duke of Normandy: 82
Robin Hood: *99*
Roman Catholic Church. *See* Catholic Church
Roman Empire: 13; collapse of, 8, 18
Rose window (Chartres Cathedral): *156*
Rupertsberg (convent): *22, 24*

S

Sacraments: *30*, 31, *32-33*
Saint-Denis: 33, 38-40
Saint-Germain des Prés: 89-95
Saint John's Eve: 104
Saint Peter's basilica: 15-16; Charlemagne in, *14*
Saladin (Muslim leader): 87
Saladin, Matilda: 99
Saladin, Philip: 99
Samhain: 103
Santiago de Compostela: and pilgrimage to, 34-*35; map* 35
Saracens. *See* Muslims
Scallop shell, from Santiago pilgrimage: *34, 35*
Scientific method: 128
Scriptorium: *46,* 130-131
Seven arts: 126
Shakespeare, William: 110
Siege warfare: *50-51*
Songs: *Carmina Burana,* 128; of courtly love, illustration from, *67;* of Hildegard von Bingen, *25*
Stained-glass windows: *156-157*
Stephen (king of England): 51-52, 55-56
Steward: 92-94
Stoicism: 52

Strasbourg Cathedral: *155*
Sword, toy: *117*

T

Taverns: *104, 105*
Thieves: 123
Thomas Aquinas (saint): 11, 126
Tilt: *74*
Tournaments: *72-75;* prizes in, *75*
Toys: *117*
Trade. *See* Merchants
Translators: 131
Trivium: 126
Tura, Agnolo di: 140
Twelfth Night: 103

U

Universities: 10, 126-128, *127*
Urban II (pope): 79, *80*
Urban III (pope): 87
Urban life: *120*-147, *121, 122, 123*
Urinalysis: *96-97*
Utensils, cooking: *93*

V

Viart, Philippot: 147
Visigoths: 8

W

Walker (for child): *117*
Warfare: 10-11, 50-87; siege, *50-51*
Wars of the Roses: 106, 110
Wells Cathedral: *152-153*
White Ladies: 129
White Ship, wreck of: 54
Whitsunday: 104
William I (the Conqueror; king of England): 9, 54
William of Champeaux: 27
Women: and Christine de Pisan on, 71; laborers, 92, 95; merchants, 124; prostitutes, 129. *See also individual names*
Wood gathering and chopping: *92*
Woodwards: 98
Writing: 18, 19, 21, 25

Y

Yuletide: 103

Time-Life Books is a division of Time Life Inc.

TIME LIFE INC.
PRESIDENT and CEO: George Artandi

TIME-LIFE BOOKS
PRESIDENT: Stephen R. Frary
PUBLISHER/MANAGING EDITOR: Neil Kagan

What Life Was Like
IN THE AGE OF CHIVALRY

EDITOR: Denise Dersin
DIRECTOR, NEW PRODUCT DEVELOPMENT:
Curtis Kopf
MARKETING DIRECTORS: Pamela R. Farrell, Joseph
A. Kuna

Deputy Editor: Paula York-Soderlund
Design Director: Cynthia T. Richardson
Text Editors: James Michael Lynch, Robin Currie
Associate Editor/ Research and Writing:
Trudy W. Pearson
Senior Copyeditor: Mary Beth Oelkers-Keegan
Technical Art Specialist: John Drummond
Picture Coordinator: David Herod
Editorial Assistant: Christine Higgins

Special Contributors:
Anthony Allan, Charlotte Anker, Ellen Phillips, Daniel
Stashower (chapter text); Dale Brown, Jarelle S. Stein
(writing); Magdalena Anders, Ann Lee Bruen, Mark
Galan, Ann Greer, Patricia J. Onderko, Myrna Traylor-
Herndon, Elizabeth Schleichert, Barry N. Wolverton
(research-writing); Kristin A. Dittman, Ann-Louise Gates,
Patricia Nelson (research); Lina Baber Burton (overread);
Jennifer Rushing-Schurr (index).

Correspondents: Maria Vincenza Aloisi (Paris), Christine
Hinze (London), Christina Lieberman (New York). Valu-
able assistance was also provided by: Barbara Gevene Hertz
(Copenhagen), Angelika Lemmer (Bonn), Ann Natanson
(Rome).

Vice President, Director of Finance: Christopher Hearing
Vice President, Book Production: Marjann Caldwell
Director of Publishing Technology: Betsi McGrath
Director of Photography and Research: John Conrad Weiser
Director of Editorial Administration: Barbara Levitt
Production Manager: Marlene Zack
Quality Assurance Manager: Miriam P. Newton
Chief Librarian: Louise D. Forstall

Consultant:
Steven Fanning received his Ph.D. in medieval history
from the University of Minnesota and is associate professor
of history and assistant dean of the College of Liberal Arts
and Sciences at the University of Illinois at Chicago. He is
the author of *A Bishop and His World before the Gregorian
Reform: Hubert of Angers (1006-1047)* as well as a dozen ar-
ticles on the history of the Lombards, Anglo-Saxons,
Franks, bishops, noble families, and political theory in late
antiquity and the Middle Ages. Dr. Fanning has also contributed entries to the *Dictionary of the Middle Ages; Medieval France, An Encyclopedia;* and the *Readers Companion to
Military History.* He is currently working on studies of
kingship and emperorship in the Roman Empire and the
early Middle Ages as well as medieval mysticism.

First printing. Printed in U.S.A.
School and library distribution by Time-Life Education,
P.O. Box 85026, Richmond, Virginia 23285-5026.

Time Life is a trademark of Time Warner Inc. U.S.A.

Library of Congress Cataloging-in-Publication Data
What Life Was Like In the Age of Chivalry: Medieval Europe, AD 800-1500/by the editors of Time-Life Books.
      p. cm.
      Includes bibliographical references and index.
      ISBN 0-7835-5451-6
      1. Civilization, Medieval. 2. Chivalry. 3. Manners
and customs—History. 4. Social history—Medieval, 500-
1500. I. Time-Life Books.
CB353.W47 1997   97-13092
940.1—dc21   CIP

Other Publications:
HISTORY
The American Story
Voices of the Civil War
The American Indians
Lost Civilizations
Mysteries of the Unknown
Time Frame
The Civil War
Cultural Atlas

COOKING
Weight Watchers® Smart Choice Recipe Collection
Great Taste~Low Fat
Williams-Sonoma Kitchen Library

SCIENCE/NATURE
Voyage Through the Universe

DO IT YOURSELF
The Time-Life Complete Gardener
Home Repair and Improvement
The Art of Woodworking
Fix It Yourself

TIME-LIFE KIDS
Family Time Bible Stories
Library of First Questions and Answers
A Child's First Library of Learning
I Love Math
Nature Company Discoveries
Understanding Science & Nature

For information on and a full description of any of the
Time-Life Books series listed above,
please call 1-800-621-7026 or write:

Reader Information
Time-Life Customer Service
P.O. Box C-32068
Richmond, Virginia 23261-2068

This volume is one in a series on world history that uses
contemporary art, artifacts, and personal accounts to
create an intimate portrait of daily life in the past.

Other volumes included in the
What Life Was Like series:

On the Banks of the Nile: Egypt, 3050-30 BC
When Rome Ruled the World: The Roman Empire, 100 BC- AD 200
At the Dawn of Democracy: Classical Athens, 508-322 BC
When Longships Sailed: Vikings, AD 800-1100